URBAN PROFESSIONALS
AND THE
FUTURE OF THE METROPOLIS

Kennikat Press
National University Publications
Interdisciplinary Urban Series

General Editor
Raymond A. Mohl
Florida Atlantic University

URBAN PROFESSIONALS

AND THE

FUTURE OF THE
METROPOLIS

Edited by
PAULA DUBECK and ZANE L. MILLER

National University Publications
KENNIKAT PRESS // 1980
Port Washington, N.Y. // London

Manufactured in the United States of America

Published by
Kennikat Press Corp.
Port Washington, N.Y. / London

Library of Congress Cataloging in Publication Data

Main entry under title:

Urban professionals and the future of the metropolis.

(Interdisciplinary urban series)
Papers from four symposia sponsored by the University of Cincinnati.
Bibliography: p.
Includes index.
1. Urban policy—United States—Addresses, essays, lectures. 2. Housing policy—United States—Addresses, essays, lectures. 3. Medical policy—United States—Addresses, essays, lectures. I. Miller, Zane L. II. Dubeck, Paula J., 1944-   III. Cincinnati. University.
HT123.U76   307.7'6'0973   79-29748
ISBN 0-8046-9261-0

CONTENTS

PREFACE

This book, a product of four symposia sponsored by the University of Cincinnati in connection with the bicentennial of the American Revolution, contains essays by historians and by specialists in housing and health care. Although these essays were prepared in the middle of the 1970s, we think that for several reasons they deserve the attention of both urban professionals generally and interested lay readers. First, the problems addressed by our essayists are still with us, and in essentially the same form and context as in that bicentennial year. Second, many of the essays raise ethical and moral questions of general rather than particular interest. Third, the editors have sought in their introductory materials and in their conclusion to raise issues about the role of urban professionals as a group in determining the future of the metropolis and about the nature of the crisis that afflicts the various academic disciplines related to public policy formation in metropolitan areas.

When President Carter presented his national urban policy, the "urban crisis" no longer seemed confined to the largest metropolitan areas in the Northeast and Midwest. By the late 1970s, familiar problems in the larger metropolitan areas of those regions seemed common in the smaller ones, and in 1979 the United States Conference of Mayors criticized the Carter proposal by calling for federal assistance to prosperous cities of the "sunbelt," such as San Antonio, Houston, and Phoenix, in dealing with their "pockets of poverty." In all these places, unemployment and housing needs preoccupied local officials, and throughout the Northeast and Midwest, fiscal crunches contributed to the persisting sense of crisis.

President Carter's policy was intended to provide a "comprehensive, long-term commitment to the Nation's urban areas," and a number of themes ran through his message: the federal government cannot solve urban problems alone; blanket programs do not necessarily provide effective solutions to problems; there is an increasing resistance to federal control over local matters. President Carter's proposed policy addressed these themes through its emphasis on forging a "new partnership" between private industry and government and between federal, state, and local governments, and through more rigorous program evaluation and the targeting of those areas that most need assistance. In proposing this "new partnership," Carter's urban program relied upon corporate strategies of accountability and program evaluation while attempting to bring new economic life to distressed areas by providing federal incentives in the form of grants, tax credits, and subsidies for localities that join the effort. Underlying this policy rested the "trickle-down" theory of economic development: increased private investment would create more permanent jobs, thereby securing an increased tax base for particular areas and enhancing the fiscal capability of local governments to provide amenities for building more livable cities.

The nature of the livable city was not defined, however, except as it was linked to economic viability. While acknowledging the importance of local economic development and long-term employment, Carter's critics have argued that he has failed to deal with those very problems that people identify as necessary to resolve in order to make cities livable: high taxes, crime, soaring labor costs, and poor schools. And while few argue with Carter's contention that the city must survive if the metropolitan area is to survive, the magnitude and source of support he proposed for the survival of cities has generated considerable argument. Some have complained that the program will fall flat from too little commitment of funds; others suggest little support for the policy will emerge because it ignores those areas expected to provide most of the funding—the suburbs and the sunbelt.

In any case, it seems unlikely that Carter's policy will become a new national urban policy. At the moment, major elements of the policy are stalled in Congress. And although the proposed policy does not call for a financial outlay that is anywhere near the magnitude of President Johnson's Great Society programs, fiscal issues provide a major stumbling block to the passage of key elements of the policy. Through the legislative process, a piecemeal approach seems once more likely to inhibit the establishment of a national urban policy.

How these factors are to be addressed brings us to the issue of the role of the urban professional. While Carter's policy makes the professional accountable for the effectiveness of various urban programs, these are essentially technical problems. What remains unexplored are the professional's basic assumptions about the nature of the metropolis of the future, assumptions that underlie the policies and programs of urban professionals as they seek to enhance the quality of life of the residents of our cities. And beyond that rests the question of the appropriateness of permitting urban professionals to play such a dominant role in both the making and implementation of urban policy. Because there are no easy answers to these questions, we have collected these essays in the hope of advancing the discussion about the future of the metropolis and the role of the urban professional in its development.

We should like to acknowledge the assistance of several individuals in making this book possible. Dr. Lawrence C. Hawkins, Vice-President of Metropolitan Affairs at the University of Cincinnati at the time of the symposium, provided assistance in planning and financing the symposium. His Metropolitan Advisory Council helped organize the sessions, as did the university's Council on Academic Urban Programs. Since 1976, Dr. Calvert Smith, Vice-Provost for Continuing Education and Metropolitan Affairs, has patiently encouraged us to bring out the book, and the Council on Academic Urban Affairs has given us steadfast encouragement and support. The departments of Sociology and History at the University of Cincinnati have given us the time and resources to pull the material together. Without the aid of all those people and units, this volume would not have been possible.

Paula J. Dubeck
Zane L. Miller

URBAN PROFESSIONALS
AND THE
FUTURE OF THE METROPOLIS

CONTRIBUTORS

Paula J. Dubeck, Assistant Professor of Sociology, University of Cincinnati

Barry D. Karl, Professor of History, University of Chicago

William L. Kissick, Professor of Community Medicine, University of Pennsylvania School of Medicine

John McKnight, Associate Director, Center for Urban Affairs, Northwestern University

Zane L. Miller, Professor of History, University of Cincinnati

Malcolm L. Peterson, Office of the Vice-President, University of Washington Health Sciences Center

Richard C. Wade, Professor of History, Graduate Center, City University of New York

Jacob B. Ward, Lawyer, Member of the Conciliation and Appeals Board, New York City

Sam Bass Warner, Jr., Professor of History, Boston University

Grace Ziem, Associate Professor of Health Services and Health Care Organization, School of Health Services, The Johns Hopkins University

PAULA DUBECK & ZANE L. MILLER

During the fall of 1975, as New York City teetered on the brink of municipal insolvency and as officials in Boston and Louisville watched their cities lapse into violence over the question of busing, the University of Cincinnati called together a group of "urban professionals," including scholars as well as public and private-sector persons with special expertise in urban affairs. The occasion was the first of a four-session symposium entitled "The Future of the Metropolis." Though planned well in advance of the particular outbreak of unpleasantness that plagued several cities in 1975, the event coincided with a renewal of a sense of urban crisis that dominated serious thinking about American cities during the 1960s. That mood helped secure the enactment of a flurry of urban legislation proposed by President Lyndon B. Johnson and the creation of the federal Urban Affairs Council in 1969 to "advise and assist" then President Richard M. Nixon "in the development of a national urban policy," a step that represented the first official act of the Nixon presidency. By 1972, however, the Nixon administration had called a moratorium on the urban crisis. With the public preoccupied first by his flirtation with China and then by his gradual slide into the Watergate morass, President Nixon dismantled much of the federal machinery assembled during the Kennedy-Johnson years to aid the nation's great cities. But by 1975 the perception of energy and resource shortages after the Arab-Israeli war of 1973, followed by "stagflation," widespread municipal fiscal difficulties, general recognition of the decay of the urban-industrial heartland, and the emergence of the sunbelt as the region of liveliest metropolitan growth, growing concern about the country's health-care delivery system and the persistence of familiar housing and racial problems, made it respectable once more to view the condition of huge cities with alarm. In that context, we organized the 1975 symposium.

Conveners of the symposium charged those who delivered papers with a conventional assignment. New conditions seemed to warrant a reassessment of the nature and direction of urban growth and of urban policy. Specifically, the call to the conference cited energy and resource shortages, a reversal of the trend of south-to-north migration of blacks, the neighborhood-organization revolution, the revival of ethnic consciousness, and the advent of an era of zero-population growth as fundamental factors with potentially profound consequences for the structure and tone of metropolitan life during the last quarter of the twentieth century. Beyond that, however, the sponsors of the symposium gave its featured speakers a free hand, hoping fervently that the call, issued in the context of urban crisis reborn, would suffice as an organizing strand to evoke a measure of coherence for the four sessions. Surprisingly, perhaps, a focus did emerge, though its locus proved unexpected. While the papers addressed from various angels the issues raised in the call, they shared in common a distrust amounting almost to disrespect for the post-World War II performance of "urban professionals."

The spectacle of urban professionals attacking their own kind reminded us of another dimension of the crisis mood of the 1960s, one capitalized upon in national politics by George C. Wallace, who built his career as a potent third-party threat in part by persistently haranguing the dictatorial arrogance of "pointy-headed intellectuals" and "brief-case toting bureaucrats." By the mid-1970s, however, the fear and distrust of urban professionals among the masses, which got some play in the 1960s among young "radical" members of professional organizations protesting the dominance of their groups by well-entrenched "old boy" networks, had filtered up to a substantial portion of those establishmentarian professionals from among whose ranks came the dispensers of now vilified urban programs. Only now the discontent, as expressed by our speakers, possessed not only a common target but a common theoretical complaint. The varied analyses of the urban condition at the Cincinnati symposium centered less on the sins of politicians or the need to control more effectively vast economic, social, or demographic forces and movements than they did on the failure of the professionally tailored urban policies of the past generation. And the criticism tended to attack those policies less for their technical errors than for the inadequacy of their general perspective, their failure to espouse a broad rather than a narrow approach to problems, their inability, despite their commitment to the rhetoric of metropolitan interdependence, to develop anything more than piecemeal and partial programs for specific "problems" rather than an integrated urban policy informed by a clear sense of priorities.

Ironically, the papers at the symposium, to the extent that they bore any coherence, identified the same central issue in the crisis of the mid-1970s as did another urban professional, Daniel Patrick Moynihan, on the eve of his departure for Washington in the late 1960s to take up the position of Assistant to the President for Urban Affairs. Unlike them, however, Moynihan proposed a strangely old-fashioned solution. In an essay measuring the roots of the malaise, Moynihan ticked off six continuing themes in American urban history—violence, migration, wealth, mobility, intellectual antiurbanism, and ugliness—discounting each therefore as the source of the current crisis. He then turned to a castigation of twentieth-century technology, closing it by quoting Lewis Mumford on the need for

a reorientation in the purposes and ultimate ideals of our whole civilization—solutions that hinge on a change of mind, as far-reaching as that which characterized the changes from the medieval religious mind to the modern scientific mind. So far from looking to a scientifically oriented technology to solve our problems, we must realize that this highly sophisticated dehumanized technology itself now produces some of our most vexatious problems.[1]

And to make the crux of the crisis more specific, Moynihan cited James Q. Wilson and Edward C. Banfield, whose research identified "a sense of the failure of community" as that difficulty which "constituted the 'urban' problem for a large percentage (perhaps a majority) of urban citizens." As a solution Moynihan proposed "something more than thinking," and nothing less than a change of heart, a "certain giving of ourselves with no certainty of what will come of it. It is the only way, and imperfectly known at that."

This sort of "moral" dissatisfaction among urban professionals about urban policy is not, of course, a phenomenon peculiar to the 1960s and 1970s. It appeared almost simultaneously with the emergence of the urban professionals as a self-conscious group in the early decades of this century. It stemmed then from a new conception of the city. Down to about the first quarter of the nineteenth century, the English-speaking world saw cities as commercial communities, corporate devices for the organization and regulation of the economy. During the early part of the nineteenth century, the view of the municipal corporation as a mechanism for economic regulation disappeared, replaced by a definition that treated cities as residential communities, mere agglomerations of people and institutions for whose needs the municipality developed services to make competing urban areas pleasant places in which to live. By the early twentieth century, however, that formulation gave way to a conception of the city as an organic community comprised of differentiated parts working together for the good of the whole.

It was this conception that dominated the thought of the first generation of academic urban sociologists, whose theoretical work influenced so profoundly the new professionals in health care, social work, public administration, and city planning. The first-generation urban professionals disdained the efforts of amateur reformers who, as Professor Ernest W. Burgess of the "Chicago school" of urban sociologists expressed it in 1926, had turned the city into

the "happy hunting ground" of movements: the better-government movement, the social-work movement, the public-health movement, the playground movement, the social-center movement, the settlement movement, the Americanization movement. All these movements, lacking a basic understanding or conception of the city, have relied upon administrative devices, for the most part, to correct the evils of city life. Even the community organization movement, theoretically grounded upon a conception of the city as a unit, had the misfortune to stake its program upon an assumption of the supreme value of the revival of the neighborhood in the city instead of upon a pragmatic, experimental program guided by studies of actual conditions and trends in urban life.[2]

The perception of the city as an organic community, and the split between urban professionals and amateur reformers which appeared in the 1920s, persisted through three decades. It underlay the nature and the reception accorded Roderick D. McKenzie's book, *The Metropolitan Community* (1933), written by the University of Michigan sociologist at the behest of President Herbert Hoover's Research Committee on Social Trends. McKenzie cited the automobile as the great "disturbing" force responsible for social disorganization in the nation's cities, but the book failed to dissuade the committee or the Hoover administration from treating the city as "a tail to the economic kite" and therefore inhibited the composing of an urban policy. The same thing happened during the New Deal. To be sure, the green-belt town program bore the marks of influence by the urban professionals, but only three of the new towns—scarely enough to constitute a national urban policy—ever materialized. More significantly, when FDR's National Resources Board appointed an Urbanism Committee to study "the role of the urban community in the national economy," the final report inverted the equation and talked more about restoring the health of the national economy than solutions for the sickness of the urban community. And the reconstruction of cities after World War II, which drew heavily on federal aid and which "amateurs" hailed as an "urban renaissance," also centered on "programs," such as public housing and downtown renewal, that treated urban problems as discrete phenomena rather than as malfunctions of the delicate tissue of urban community considered as a unit.

Still, despite the popular acclaim accorded the "urban renaissance" of the 1950s, the sense of crisis among urban professionals persisted, and they tried once more during the 1960s, this time with more influence, to inform national policy on cities with their perspective. In 1965, President Johnson, declaring that the "modern city can be the most ruthless enemy of the good life, or it can be its servant," made the resolution of urban problems a centerpiece in the Great Society by signing an act establishing the Department of Housing and Urban Development. He did so, moreover, in response to the importuning of professionals who, before the long hot summers of rioting in the latter years of the decade, convinced almost everybody that the cities stood in deep trouble. When Johnson acted, however, the urban professionals themselves had adopted a theoretical stance toward "the urban community" which inhibited the development of a national urban policy of the sort envisaged by most of those who presented papers at the Cincinnati symposium.

By the 1960s few urban professionals spoke the language of Burgess, Mumford, or even Moynihan. Instead, they had replaced the organic conception of the city with a more mechanistic one, considering it as a system composed of individuals and organizations whose competition tended toward a dynamic equilibrium. Cities now seemed "communities of limited liability," in Morris Janowitz's felicitous phrase, and in them people made only partial and short-term commitments to localities, moving freely and frequently as career opportunities and changing cultural tastes and life-cycle stages dictated. That perspective suggested a policy favoring the creation of a nation of diverse yet essentially interchangeable communities equal in the services and amenities they offered their inhabitants. That view was expressed explicitly in 1964 in the report of President

Johnson's Task Force on Metropolitan and Urban Problems, a group dominated by the new-breed urban professionals and whose report provided the foundation for the Great Society's urban policies. "The provision of choices in social, economic and political life," the Task Force contended, "is the prime function of the great urban community. Now that the United States is a nation of cities of all sorts and sizes, the maintenance of free choices for its citizens is an increasingly complex affair. But the need to ensure options in choice of residence, place of work, meaningful leisure-time activities, and effective civic participation was never greater."[3] Johnson himself drove the point home in his 1965 special message to Congress on "the Nation's Cities," which prefaced his proposals for improving the quality of urban life, particularly in its residential aspects.

We must extend the range of choices available to all our people so that all, and just not the fortunate, can have access to decent homes and schools, to recreation and to culture. . . . The American city should be a collection of communities where every member has a right to belong. It should be a place where every man feels safe on his streets and in the house of his friends. It should be a place where each individual's dignity and self-respect is strengthened by the respect and affection of his neighbors. It should be a place where each of us can find the satisfaction and warmth which comes only from being a member of the community of man.[4]

Such a shotgun approach might have worked, given time and plentiful financial support. But it never really had a chance. Congress adopted only parts of the package, and the Nixon administration, which ultimately struck a posture of benign neglect both toward the issue of race and the big cities, eventually undid those. In the late 1970s, moreover, the disappearance of the fundamental assumption of abundance and unlimited economic growth makes it unlikely that the Carter administration and its successors will adopt anything resembling a program to promote the revival of the community of limited liability. The speakers at the Cincinnati symposia, needless to add, came up with few solutions to particular metropolitan problems, but their unanticipated concentration on the shortcomings of the general perspective with which urban professionals work pointed to a central difficulty. Before dealing adequately with specific problems, their critiques suggested, we need to develop a new conception of urban community, one capable of sustaining a balanced and discriminating national urban policy based upon a careful analysis and assessment of the legacies of the past, the new stringencies of our times, and realistic prospects of the future.

This volume, then, is addressed to a broad audience of students, policy makers, and civic leaders, professionals and lay persons alike, with an abiding interest in urban affairs and the future of the metropolis. Clearly, that group must first face such immediate concerns as the fiscal integrity of cities. But it must also look to the long run. It must consider the source and appropriate uses of scarce energy and material and capital resources; the influence of population changes on neighborhoods, housing, and the economy; the provision of high-quality social services demanded by citizens accustomed to the highest standard of living on the globe; and the growth of ethnic and neighborhood consciousness in big-city communities and suburbs alike. Before even beginning the discussion of these concerns, however, three more basic questions must be posed: What kind of metropolis do we want for the future? What kind of future can we expect in light of our current predicament? In the absence of a neat fit, to what extent and how can we bring our aspirations into line with our possibilities? And fundamental to each remains the most critical question of all: Who shall decide, and how? The answers to these questions will determine the future of the metropolis. We think the essays that follow establish a unique point of departure from which to proceed with the search.

NOTES

1. Daniel P. Moynihan, "The City in Chassis," in Daniel P. Moynihan, ed., *Toward a National Urban Policy* (New York, 1970), pp. 334–336.
2. Ernest W. Burgess, ed., *The Urban Community* (Chicago, 1926), p. viii.
3. Mark I. Gelfand, *A Nation of Cities* (New York, 1975), pp. 367–368.
4. Ibid., p. 370.

PART ONE

THE URBAN PROFESSIONAL:
Conventional Wisdom Reexamined

THE EDITORS

OVERVIEW AND PREVIEW

In planning for the future, we generally follow one of two courses. We either predict from the present to the future, on a step-by-step basis, or we designate some desirable future and work back from that point to the present, defining activities which would carry us to that end. The first procedure is limited by our ability to predict the future with relative accuracy. We have little difficulty predicting short-term events, yet beyond this, we falter because of insufficient information about the consequences of as well as the impact of unanticipated events on our initial decisions. The second approach seems more attractive and satisfying because some specific objective has been formulated and provides a base line against which to measure our progress. While limited by techniques to engineer mediating states, it at least gives us direction even in the event that one of our chosen activities temporarily diverts us from our goal. This kind of planning, focusing on an end point, requires that we define what is desirable and that we assign priorities among those things desired. These later considerations are the issues addressed in the first set of articles on urban professionals and the future of the metropolis.

One problem of defining goals for the future—a process which of necessity deals with concepts rather than concrete circumstances—is their ambiguity. Today goals for the future often come summarized in catch-all phrases, none of them more popular than "the quality of life." But what does this phrase mean to urban planners and citizens and to the politicians who ultimately make decisions determining the quality of life? In a recent article, Elihu M. Gerson outlined the two traditional perspectives on the fundamental issue involved in determining quality of life.[1] The first, focusing on individual achievement, approaches quality of life in terms of the "degree to which an individual accomplishes his desires," and thereby places a general emphasis on the dominance of the individual over society. The other reverses that tendency. It focuses on social stability, defining quality of life in terms of the "degree to which the individual carries out his place in the larger social order." At one end of this spectrum stands anarchy; at the other, totalitarianism.

Gerson proposes to extricate us from that dilemma by arguing that the polarity is neither necessary nor realistic. The older modes of thinking, he contends, are inappropriate because each starts by separating individuals from their "containing social order," a step that pits component parts of the social order (individuals) against society when in fact they are one. Starting with the inseparability of man and society, Gerson suggests that we look at patterns of interaction among people with special reference to social relationships as the key ingredient in conceptualizing the nature of the quality of life.

As it turns out, social relationships in urban life have been of continuing interest to historians, sociologists, and other social scientists throughout the twentieth century. Although not all of them used the phrase "quality of life," many students of the city addressed fundamental questions of goodness, serenity, stability, justice, and intimacy. Some despaired over the breakdown of traditional family ties, the dissolution of neighborliness, and the erosion of standards of behavior that seemingly accompanied the emergence of the large, dense, heterogeneous settlements of people we think of as modern urban areas. This group saw even those structures originally expected to compensate for individual and social fragmentation as inadequate to the task. On the other hand, some applauded the variety and diversity they saw as endemic to modern urban growth. In their perspective, varied populations provided the raw materials for creativity and the appearance of unique special interests and of structures that augmented the role of the individual in political decisions. To them, as Frederick Howe put it at the turn of the century, the city seemed "the hope of democracy."

Outside these two dominant camps, and more recent in their origins, stand advocates of two other positions. One group, attaching little in the way of "morality" to the process of urbanization, regarded urban growth and its corresponding social forms as "natural" events, not unlike the biological processes common among all orders of living things. Another rather similar but less naturalistic and deterministic group centered its attention on the mobility of individuals and the meaning of that for the local community rather than for the urban community. While this latter school concluded that the modern metropolis consists of "communities of limited liability" through which people move in response to changing career patterns and stages in their life cycles, a quest for something called "community" characterized each shift of residence.

Like the peripatetic inhabitants of contemporary communities of limited liability, exponents of the four major approaches to the nature of urban life in the twentieth century have shared a concern with "community." Though their definitions of that elusive concept varied in detail, they all perceived it as a place or locale, however ill-defined, bound together by behavioral norms. Such units, as Minar and Greer expressed it, possess "aspects which are valued if they exist, desired in their absence."

Community is indivisible from human actions, purposes, and values. It expresses our vague yearnings for a commonality of desires, a communion with those around us, and extension of the bonds of kin and friend to all those who share a common fate with us.[2]

Seen in that light, the attempt to create "community" describes a mode of behavior corresponding with the way people relate to each other outside the connections demanded by functional necessity. But community is at the same time and of necessity bounded and exclusionary. The broader the area encompassed by the community, the less intimate and concrete is one's experience of the communal feeling. Consequently, individuals impulsively establish limits in an effort to create a community's identity, a process that simultaneously defines those without as well as those within the community. Therein lies the rub, for the exclusionary nature of community runs headlong into the pressure for change as the present slips inevitably into the future and erodes the idealized stability that, however temporary, undergirds the concept of community in any of its formulations.

This pressure for change is axiomatic. What is not axiomatic are the kinds of changes that will occur and how they will be managed. Taking into account the inertia of history and recognizing the importance of ideas as stimuli to action suggests that the future we face is neither wholly out of our control nor completely within it. That future will surely be shaped by us, and particularly by our efforts to define the attributes of urban living which we deem necessary to provide a satisfying existence for the future inhabitants of the metropolis. What, then, *are* the desired qualities of urban life? It is, in short, our own goals that constitute the fundamental problems for the planner, the politician, and the citizen.

In the first of the set of articles in this section, Barry D. Karl introduces us to the historical role of the first generation of urban professionals and their distinctive vision. Karl argues that professionalism and morality in the early twentieth century were congruent and compatible approaches to community order because of the planners' confidence in the persistence of their basic values into the future. He suggests, however, that today's planners hold a scientifically objective and essentially amoral view of urbanization and society, a view that lacks a vision to direct change, a view devoid of a sense of "afterlife" reflecting *faith* in the future of the metropolis as a humane, just, democratic, and coherent environment. It is the absence of this factor that makes it possible to think that the metropolis may not have a future, for only the possession of a compelling sense of morality based on confidence in the long-range validity of our values can prepare us to deal with the future of the metropolis. In raising the issue of vision, Karl forces us to recognize that all planning, regardless of its pretensions to objective professionalism, is value-laden, and that to establish and choose those kinds of goals toward which to work must be the first order of business if there is to be a viable future for the metropolis.

In urban areas, as perhaps nowhere else, the problem of choosing is magnified by the broad variety of interest groups and the competition among them for resources to meet their conflicting needs. In the past, we have approached—evaded may be the better word—this difficulty by assuming the availability of unlimited resources for our exploitation. The source of this strategy may be traced to the "frontier" ethos, which not only defined new challenges but also posited new and seemingly infinite resources that could be transformed for consumption in our mushrooming cities. More recently, that strategy has been bolstered by the role of technology in stimulating the economic growth which for most of the past thirty years allowed us to expand the boundaries of the metropolis and to "solve" such problems as crowded housing, inadequate schools, and transportation by expanding accessibility to the urban core and by relocating industrial and service centers. This "solution" aimed less at handling existing problems than at breaking new ground in the hope that familiar problems would either disappear or at least seem less pressing. And for most, they did seem less pressing, both physically and psychologically. The ability to move from areas of crowded housing, for example, was supported by an expanding economy and a home-mortgage system that helped young middle-income families to move to outer-city neighborhoods or the suburbs. There they lived a safe social and psychological distance from the strains of central-city life and the threat to the social order that those strains generated. Those left behind also benefited from the expanded stock of private and public housing available for use as shelter by them. Urban areas thus experienced at once an expansion of their boundaries and a decrease in density at the center.

But the unlimited-resources "solution" disappeared with the rapidly increasing cost of energy, heightened foreign competition for basic materials, the appearance of a no or slow-growth economy, and the onset of double-digit rates of inflation. Supplies of energy, especially oil and gas, are now computed in terms of the number of years they will last "at current rates of usage," although most who speculate on the matter recognize that the current rates of usage are unlikely to stabilize. Shortages of materials—by which is meant the amount available at a desirable price—reduced the construction of new housing because of high cost, eliminating appreciable movements of people out of the more densely populated areas of cities and creating at least a temporary increase in the doubling-up of families in some metropolitan areas.

Today we face the familiar problems of housing, jobs, health care, and transportation in the context of limited known and available resources and with a tempered optimism about economic growth. Do we have a vision of the future that includes limited resources? What are the constraints upon a plan concerned with the quality of life under these more modest circumstances? In the second of this set of articles, John McKnight addresses these questions by focusing on the needs of the neighborhoods. Foremost among his concerns is the need for justice and equality—items at least conceded necessary and useful in times of abundance—particularly the nagging question of racial equality. Contending that even poorer neighborhoods benefit to at least some extent during prosperity, McKnight asks us to confront the politics of distributing less. How can scarce resources be equitably shared? Must the neighborhood be allocated legal autonomy to assure the just and evenhanded distribution of limited resources? In raising these questions he also, like Karl, asks us to evaluate the past and present roles of the planners and the politicians and to assess their contributions to assuring justice and equality among the component parts of the urban body politic.

McKnight at best expresses a guarded optimism about the future of the metropolis, a reflection of how limited resources may influence the alternatives we envisage and realize during the last quarter of the twentieth century. This framework for the delivery of services and the redistribution of public wealth throughout the metropolis is one with which we are most familiar. But the framework itself may be one of the limitations on the resources with which we deal. Specifically, if resources are limited by what we perceive as available through the established system, then the economic welfare of the local area will be limited by local tax revenues and federal tax monies poured back in the community. By this arrangement public services depend upon traditional methods of assuring economic growth and on traditional means for translating private wealth into resources for meeting public needs.

In the third article, Sam Bass Warner, Jr., asks us to question these traditional assumptions. He asserts that in their abundance of public goods "metropolitan economies of the nation possess the seeds of their own rejuvenation." His focus is on potentially profitable, but now barren, urban land, and on businesses handling "universal" goods which are themselves the profitable public services and products of the habit of metropolitan living. By transferring these from the control of the private to the public sector, their profits could be harnessed to provide for the maintenance and development of metropolitan areas in a more just and equitable fashion. His aim is to prevent the poverties of the past from becoming the more severe poverties of the future, and he dangles before the beleaguered metropolis of today a method for generating new resources to enhance the quality of urban life, a method that by implication would build on itself in such a fashion as to render the idea of "limited economic resources" irrelevant. But does even this resolve the central problem of the shaping of the future? Whether the issue of limited resources is critical, or in Warner's formulation, peripheral, the issues raised by Karl and McKnight remain. But Warner's analysis pushes them to the top of the list of questions to be answered if the future of the metropolis is to be assured.

NOTES

1. Elihu M. Gerson, "On 'Quality of Life,' " *American Sociological Review*, Vol. 41, No. 5 (October 1976), pp. 793–806.
2. David W. Minar and Scott Green, *The Concept of Community: Readings with Interpretations* (Chicago, 1969), p. ix.

BARRY D. KARL

THE URBAN PROFESSIONAL AND THE
PROMISE OF LIFE AFTER DEATH

Among the various science-fiction accounts of the future urban condition, one type in particular fascinates me. It describes a citizenry re-
processed by a master computer capable of reincarnating generations faced
with the same problems, excited by the same solutions, inured to the
same failures. They repeat their experiences over and over, celebrating
their triumphs and their defeats with what appears to be the same
enthusiasm as they tell one another that acceptance of the things one can
do nothing about is itself a kind of triumph. What gives the idea its rich-
ness, of course, is the possibility that we may already be there. While our
reform enthusiasms today appear to be in a period of decline, historical
experience would suggest that another wave is bound to be on the way.
After all, the history of urban reform and speculation about life after
death do share at least one thing in common. The hard evidence thus far
accumulated has had little effect on the persistence of belief, one way
or the other. We have had urban reform ever since we have had cities
to reform.

Many of the debates are by now familiar, having already established a
history of recurrence at least as old as our national history. One basic
question seems to me a constant: what is the relation between democratic
government and the technical requirements of a highly industrialized,
specialized society? The argument often centers on pairs of terms: the
amateur versus the expert, the politician versus the administrator, the
practitioner versus the theoretician. Indeed, the classical issue of relating
theory to practice is so old now that it might seem foolish to suggest that

one could say anything new about it. There are points, however, where the expression of the problem changes so gradually that some restatement might be useful, and I should like to try.

The emergence of the professional in urban reform is a phenomenon distinct from either the growth of specialized skills in urban management or the practices of urban politics, though it is related to both. In the earlier part of the nineteenth century the urban professional—as distinct from the urban politician or the urban citizen—was someone whose special skills in medicine, sanitation, engineering, or law could be brought to the service of the city; but the technical skill was urban only in the sense that the technician was a city dweller whose sense of responsibility and whose consciousness of the effects of urbanization on the daily exercise of his profession led him to seek public action in dealing with his problems. Such professionals established a specialized literature through which they communicated their findings to one another, urged improvements, and sought to influence experiments in new methods and techniques. Their science was often simplistic, consisting of statistics, cartography, and such theses about air currents and temperature as were appropriate to pregerm-theory medicine; but their aims were consistent with the very modern notion of applying scientific methodology, rather than political expedience, to the processes of urban government.

In the three decades after the Civil War, there gradually developed an increasingly specialized concern with urban technology as requiring a separate set of skills; civil engineering, public health, public education, municipal revenues and taxation, land use, and finally the very management of the city itself became subject matters for special training in the traditional disciplines from which they had sprung. The basic apparatus of professionalism had emerged in the form of an expert literature, a system of training, and a move toward group identification through the establishment of professional associations. By the turn of the century the distinction between the management of a discipline and the intellectual pursuit of disciplinary ideas was already becoming clear, while the distinction between both and the government of the public the disciplines served sharpened. Schools of civics and philanthropy—already highly developed efforts to professionalize traditions of local charity—became schools of social work, attaching themselves to the new universities, granting advanced degrees, and certifying their graduates for specialized careers.

The professionalization of urban reform can be traced through several late-nineteenth and early-twentieth-century movements that shaped a tradition of which even this series of meetings is part. The establishment of universities in cities and the basic reorganization of older urban colleges into universities had as an important intentional base the creation of institutions for examining the city and the training of new generations for its managerial elite. Thus, Seth Low, president of Columbia, New York philanthropist and political leader, reorganized Columbia partly under pressures to make it the training ground of an urban laboratory. Many of the same ambitions underlay the founding of the University of Chicago. Robert S. Brookings expanded Washington University for St. Louis. All three institutions—Columbia, Chicago, and Washington University— were moved from their original downtown locations to spacious suburban lands where the new founding elite had resettled, assured that their young would be close enough to urban life to utilize it, but far enough away to be protected from the turmoil. City life would be the subject of research and the object of it. The new professionals would be trained to manage scientifically reformed communities.

A parallel development concerned a different but related group of professionals who clustered in variously titled research bureaus. They, too, were concerned with the technical investigation of the city as well as with its reform; but their base was their own professional experience. They separated from and often disputed with the academics who sought to advise them. Less concerned with the training of new generations, they nonetheless depended upon the new products of the university for staff as they expanded their reform interests.

Periodic meetings, often under the auspices of local city clubs and citizen associations, brought the two groups together to debate, to educate one another, and to try to envisage the future. Politics was their enemy; science, their ally. They visited one another in their various city clubs, sharing experiences and advice, and above all, encouraging one another to greater effort.

By 1920 the transformation from reform association to professional association was well under way. While the basic method remained the same, the tone changed.

Groups like the new City Manager's Association no longer found it necessary to meet under the auspices of local elite clubs. For years Saratoga, New York, and Newport, Rhode Island, had served as meeting places for similar groups, underscoring their basic sources of support. Now the universities offered their empty classrooms and dormitories, and the urban hotel became the center for meetings migrating annually from city to city. For all such groups the outward-looking reform interest of the Progressive era was replaced by an inward-looking concern for the development of the special professional group itself. They formed committees on research, established newsletters and eventually journals, elected presidents and secretaries, to keep the flow alive in between yearly meetings.

The problem of interchange from profession to profession and discipline spurred cross-professional and cross-disciplinary efforts, such as the founding of the Social Science Research Council and the establishment of the Public Administration Clearing House; but even that focus was in its way internal, as the terms "social science" and "public administration" make clear. Without rejecting their concern with the improvement of community life, they sought to universalize their professional identity, to deny its dependence upon any one community or community elite—let alone on that still vital enemy, politics. Part of the process, of course, was simply that of nationalization as they followed business and industry in looking toward Washington, establishing offices there to engage in something they would never have been willing to call lobbying. They wanted to serve, to advise, to influence, certainly; but the difference was clear to them. It was the interest of their professions they sought to serve, not self-interest. Professionals could claim that kind of purity of motive.

Theodore Roosevelt had contributed his own religious plank to the Progressive party in his ringing announcement of his battle for the Lord; but the new professionals, among them many who had followed him in 1912, were not inclined toward that rhetoric—at least, not openly. The secular Utopianism they introduced often had echoes on how to deal with their specialized problems and seek out corps of ambitious young to continue the profession and its aims. Although the state governors had already been organized and the mayors were next on the list, their frankly political status made them the audience for the new professionals. Their organization served as a convenience, gathering the consumers together to be appealed to periodically by the experts, in between their concerns with politics.

The new specialists could move freely from city to city, secure in the growing universality of their skills and the standards for judging them. All cities built on hilly terrain had similar problems of sanitation, sewage, and water supply, so the engineers of San Francisco, Providence, and Cincinnati could sit down together and discuss flows and pressures without worrying about political differences, quality of local leadership, and ethnic differences. Public health provided similar universality. There was indeed no field of public service not capable of technical improvement by being moved to a level of generalization above the murky ground of particular local dispute.

A new mobility implied a hierarchy of posts as urban professionals arranged cities on scales and ladders of opportunity, and shifted from city to city as they improved their professional status or recouped a loss from a previous post. Both possibilities formed a part of the gossip at the yearly meetings as they discussed the private state of the profession with one another. The New Deal accelerated their national mobility as they centered their attention on Washington, moving in and out of government agencies as advisers, managers, supplicants, and critics, but all in all, making possible a flow of services out of Washington that would have been considerably less efficient without them. From their classroom podiums at Harvard, Columbia, and the University of Chicago, they were training a new generation of experts in public management. They took the railroad system's elegant limiteds to Washington to give their advice and even vacated their library retreats for seasons of service in national management—working vacations from the real business of their lives. Their model was the business executive, purified of his commitment to profit and reeducated to a kind of gentlemanly Veblenianism. An occasional congressman or news analyst would discover their funding by one or more of the country's private philanthropic foundations and grumble about the takeover of the country by Standard Oil; but, by and large, a confidence in scientific knowledge supported local and national brain trusts as no other trusts had ever been supported.

The shrewdest among the new professionals did not reject politics; but they did shift their energy from a reliance on a politics based on faith in the power of popular intelligence to a reliance on a politics based on techniques in the management of attitudes and beliefs. Public-opinion polling and consumer attitudinal study moved toward modernity in their analyses. They talked rather guardedly about "social control" but were nonetheless startled at the emergence of the role of the professional public-relations expert in politics. And even then, they tended not to recognize the relation between the social sciences they were struggling to perfect and apply, and the techniques they so freely and critically associated with Madison Avenue. What was emerging in the thirties became the norm of the period after World War II, as the proliferating social involvement of the federal government in policy planning in the city and state required an expanding local bureaucracy of professionals who knew the labyrinthine passages of Washington at least as well as they knew the maps of their own communities, possibly even better, given the relative costs of losing one's way at home or abroad. Bringing local policy needs into line with available federal funding became the key technical skill. No one seemed to notice that the intention implied by that skill was exactly the opposite of the intention of the first new professionals as they converged on New Deal Washington, although that may be putting it a bit harshly. Suffice it to say that the nationalization of the urban professional may have produced some conflicts with local needs and local traditions.

That point was in some senses recognized from a rather different perspective on the very eve of the crucial period of change. A study of the city-manager movement conducted in 1940 by Harold A. Stone, Don K. Price, and Kathryn H. Stone can be read as a classic in the transition from reform to professionalism, although like most classics, it is capable of a variety of readings. A staff of researchers examined fifty of the city-manager cities in the United States and reported in detail on nine. Their aim was to produce an evaluation of the first twenty-five years of the profession which, more than any other, had been the symbol of their development. Their conclusion bridled with a defensiveness nothing in the volume—or even in the conclusion, for that matter—quite explains. They were convinced that city managers had improved urban government; but they confessed that they could even begin to measure that improvement. Indeed, they confessed that some of their evidence might dispute their conviction. Their publisher—Public Administration Service—had its offices in a building across the street from the University of Chicago's Social Science Research Building. Carved in the bay of that building were the words of Lord Kelvin: "When you cannot measure, your knowledge is meagre and unsatisfactory." One presumes our researchers averted their eyes as they passed.

Luther Gulick, a leader of the administrative movement, was less hopeful as he surveyed Lincoln Steffens' shameful cities four decades after Steffens and puzzled at the amount of shame the urban public could bear without flinching. By the mid-fifties, however, even if a survey of many of the same cities produced even less confidence, a review of historical bossism would begin to show new promise in that once-pilloried method of urban government. Political scientists were discovering the utility of raw power, and for the second or third time in that profession's history, while historians could begin to revive some of the prime examples of that method—Boss Tweed, for example. Bossism made things work, satisfied needs; and if the trains didn't run on time, there were now airplanes, automobiles, and a burgeoning highway system to aid in the funding of local government. The career of Chicago's Richard J. Daley took off while moviegoers chuckled warmly and affectionately at Spencer Tracy's portrayal of Boston's Mayor Curley.

By the end of the decade, intellectuals switched their loyalties from Adlai Stevenson to John Kennedy because Kennedy could win and Stevenson couldn't. They quoted Kennedy's expletives to one another, described the cigar-smoking politician who accompanied his lovely wife to elegant White House musicales like some modernized version of the old Maggie and Jiggs cartoons. In political campaigns a dirty trick or two was good for a laugh and an election; a little hanky-panky, a healthy sign of the responsible exercise of real power. When the roof fell in, as we all know it did, there was at least some reason for those upon whom it fell to wonder what merciless Providence had chosen them as the object of its revenge.

If the foregoing brief run-through of the recent past smacks too much of a morality play, I am partly being misunderstood—though I can well understand why. I am talking about morality because I think the issue is essentially a moral one and must be seen that way. But I am not talking about a moral issue involving praise and blame, heroes and villains who must be separated from one another. Nor am I talking about a public morality capable of arguing that we are somehow one and all to blame for whatever we think has happened. The relation between politics and morality is too subtle and complex to be understood that way. And the use of history as a form of punishment, however eternally popular it may seem, is perhaps the most serious misuse of it.

We can take a look at the administrative generation of the 1920s and 1930s from a perspective somewhat different from the one they would have chosen for themselves and perhaps a bit closer to what we can now see as the consequences of what they did. First of all, as I have already suggested in several asides, they didn't create the idea of professionalism as the alternative to amateur or citizen involvement. Professionalism is an ancient process that, in its modern form, is characteristic of every group with skills to perfect, standards to protect, and new generations to educate. Their attempt to apply professionalism to government at all levels was a real effort to answer the major question their generation throughout the world was asking of liberal democracy: Could it govern a highly industrial, technologizing society? Their answer was a sort of yes, but. . . . One has to compare their method with those being tried in other parts of the Western World, particularly Italy, Germany, and the Soviet Union during the same period before one fixes on any answer; and that isn't easy.

They clearly believed that one could separate the professional process from the moral process, retain morality in community life and education, and transfer it to those edges of professionalism that needed it. But they also believed that there was a morality inherent in the professional process itself which the profession could sustain and protect among its own membership and teach to the young. Like Veblen's Instinct for Workmanship, professional morality was a deep commitment to a preservation of one's best and most fundamental humanity through the exercise of the profession. They assumed a necessary and supportive relation between community morality and professional morality, and up to that point I would go along. But they also tended to assume that the relationship was automatic and, most important of all, that the two could not come into conflict unless the community or the profession were in serious error. And such errors would, in their terms, be obvious.

I think we can now see the problem quite differently. A profession can establish behavior that conflicts with community interest, even though it may meet the going standards of the profession more than adequately. The community can have priorities in its interests incapable of resolution in terms of the profession's conception of its own needs. The public must now serve as guinea pig for social theories incapable of testing through any other means; but no one wants to describe it that way. We have long known in medical research that some procedures can be tested only so far under controlled laboratory conditions. A point is reached where only public use can be expected to reveal new or corrective knowledge. Even commercial aircraft must be tested for the ultimate details of safety in the same way.

The elaboration of protective standards in all such instances throws into serious conflict professional judgments and public regulation in ways the earlier generation could not have conceived possible and questions assumptions that are part of the mainstay of the American conception of public morality. No amount of cost-benefit analysis, no computerized calculation of the allowable percentage of risk, can take the place of a new understanding of and an elaboration of the moral conceptions sturdy enough to serve as the base of an intuitively acceptable system of public value. It is possible that we are never going to be able to measure the educational improvement produced by busing; but that should not be the reason for attacking the practice. Indeed, the promise that we will someday be able to measure the improvement may be what should be guarded against. If there are no reasons which can be made intelligible in moral terms, we are in serious trouble.

Efforts to reexamine the relation between professionalization and morality must take a more technical form than the developing atmosphere of hostility seems to allow. A recent study of the multinational corporation, for example, focuses on the lack of concern such corporations have for national—let alone local—needs in their pursuit of their corporate interests. However justified, the criticism, putting it on grounds of private versus public morality, may be no more useful, say, than the old trust debates of the Progressive era. The professionalization of business is, after all, part of the era we are dealing with here. The business school, the corporate training program, the shifts of key personnel from company to company, the relation between family life and business career, these are all part of the same process. What I am suggesting is that we ought to stop staring at the effects of the process and raise some useful questions about the process itself.

What I am outlining, of course, is an examination of what Robert Wiebe has called "The Search for Order," the triumph of bureaucratization and professionalism sought by the whole Progressive era. What I am questioning, however, is the degree to which we should today continue to consider that a triumph. Even as recently as a decade ago, that triumph seemed secure. There were a few writers, Edward Banfield among them, who attacked social-science professionalism as a threat to the political process, not a support of it, but the general view remained basically supportive, if not downright idolatrous. If we feel less secure after Vietnam, the Pentagon Papers, and Watergate, we may have good reason; but I think the matter still calls for better analysis than that. After all, the older generation's basic conviction that modern industrial society required a well-trained, scientifically perceptive managerial elite is harder to deny in 1975 than it was to defend in 1925. They were closer to a working popular democracy than we are, and they had the advantage of having to wait long than we do to see the consequences of their mistakes. If you will allow me an absurdly mixed metaphor, our chickens can come home to roost before the eggs are hatched—let alone counted.

A return to the old amateurism would be impossible, even if one were to argue that it would be nice. We need professionalism, and we have to have bureaucracies. What I am suggesting is that the process of bureaucratic development creates problems that need to be examined. How can one describe them?

First of all, Wiebe's nineteenth-century small-town communities were good educational communities, even if they weren't always so isolated from one another as he implies. Government and the social order, such as they were, were visible; and within a general framework of disagreement, there was often a unity supported by common ethnic origin, basic Protestantism, simple economic ambition, and a belief in constitutional government. The professionalizing generation of the 1920s carried those values with them into their urban professions. They assumed their continuity in the professions, and they assumed a basic character on which agreement about them would be sustained. It seems not to have occurred to them that loyalty to professional ideals could transcend loyalty to a community, could ultimately come into conflict with loyalty to a community. The government of the Soviet Union today is learning that there is an international literary and scientific community of which their leading citizens are members. In a different way, Americans in the 1960s and 1970s faced some of the same problems, and are today suffering some of the same confusions. Professionalization by its very nature conflicts with loyalty to other communities by providing an ideological base for a career, a sense of purpose, a definition of achievement, and a set of standards by which others in the professional community pass judgment. Can a managerial leadership committed to such professionalization move from local community to local community and provide the same leadership one sees in the preprofessional era of community development?

Secondly, professionalization was intended to protect the professional from outside attack by elaborating the standards of criticism and specifying those that were acceptable. While there was a range of such protection, including certification in some professions, the professionalizing generation did not intend that protection to be absolute or totally internal. They saw crucial distinctions between unionization and professionalism. Job security was second to the security of the profession. Tenure was defined by professional conduct, and they worked to elaborate the standards of such conduct. If they did not always see the possible breakdown of the relation between community loyalty and professional loyalty, neither did they foresee the conflict between professional interest and community interest. Their communities were intended to have the right to learn by their experiences, to change their goals, to elaborate new and innovative senses of their needs under enlightened popular direction. The professions and their bureaucracies were to serve community interest, not to control it. That essential anti-intellectualism was the core of their intellectualism, the democratic center of their professionalism. If a man or woman be selected to accomplish a certain job, and if the bureaucracy assigned to aid him or her disagrees with that aim and can show professional support for that disagreement, what rules of battle are there for determining the outcome? The Nixon presidency may be one of the most significant of this century in that respect; and we are observing a similar playing-out of problems in the city of New York. The newspaper reporter is no longer simply a reporter serving his editor; he is a professional responsible to his conception of his profession—at times even more, perhaps, than to the public; and the difficulty in telling the difference should not be as great as it now appears to be. Honesty or dishonesty may be a terribly misleading way of viewing the issue.

Finally, their professionalism was not intended to conflict with their Utopianism or, indeed, to supplant their Utopianism with a scientifically designed community. Their science was a method, not an end. Their science could not supply the substance of the dreams of the future necessary to make Utopianism useful. Yet, there is evidence that, beginning in the late 1950s, there was a general effort to replace Utopianism with method. Talk of the end of ideology was part of that movement. In 1960 McGeorge Bundy published an article on foreign policy in which he announced the end of the age of generalization. He called for a leader who could cope with the particularity of piecemeal solutions to rapidly shifting problems utilizing the evidence at hand, but also for a leader capable of convincing the public that there were larger ends and greater purposes. Few statements I know of draw a harder, blacker line between reality and Utopia, or suggest, more bleakly or more honestly, the dilemma. The President as technician versus the President as public-relations man may be one way of putting the problem, but it's not the one I prefer. The President as metaphysician and poet seems to me better, for that brings me to my conclusion.

My title and my opening both refer to life after death as though the idea were a joke. I don't think it is; but I'm not suggesting a séance. I am suggesting a problem underlying everything I have been saying. The professional generation of the 1920s and '30s was made up of people who believed in some kind of immortality and some ultimate judgment to which they had to be responsible. They tended to subject their drives for power to a moral standard they saw in popular will and in American political history. Their Utopianism rested on the belief that the American future was the future of mankind. Their pragmatism was checked always by their sense of that future. It limited the methods they were willing to use because it placed the means-end relationship in a framework established by their strong sense of constitutionalism, legalism, and human rights. If they at times acknowledged the continuing presence of injustice more privately to one another than their ideals could justify, it was always with the awareness that the future would be better, that gradualism would eventually work because that was the direction, the trend, the movement of progress. They placed a great deal of faith in their professional skills because they saw professionalism as the means toward the ultimate establishment of a great society.

Most important, perhaps, most of that generation held in some form a belief in some concept of future life where rewards and punishments would be distributed. As they became more sophisticated about the plurality of beliefs in their own community and as they acquainted themselves with the attitudes of others in their growing contacts with parts of the world they had known only through fables and myths, they moderated their faith, generalized it, but they kept it. Some translated their Protestantism directly into social science. They believed it to be self-correcting, genuinely incapable of basic misuse; and those who lived to read Thomas Kuhn's *Structure of Scientific Revolutions* heralded there the paradigm of all paradigms: that the scientific community would always have to accept the revolutions occasioned by truth, however painful its process of emergence might be. Kuhn acknowledges the resistance to change, the professional and educational apparatus not willing to be disturbed by transformations in beliefs; but I don't think he does so in ways social scientists ought so easily to accept. The truths of social science, such as they are, are found at their best in human behavior, are applied to human behavior, and may even achieve significant changes in human behavior. But we are now reaching a level of sophistication capable of arguing that not all social truth is useful truth socially. Not everything capable of producing social change ought to be tried, however useful the end might appear. Ever since the development of the atomic bomb we have been debating the utility of all experiments in nature. In educational psychology, as in atomic physics, the relation among the development of professional commitments, the need for continuing research and experiment, and the bureaucratic conflicts engendered by the process itself demand considerably more attention than they now receive. No one seems to want to describe in rational terms how dangerous the fallout from social-science experimentation might be. The issues such discussion touches once focused on why Johnny couldn't read, or add, or subtract. They now encompass the sensitive issues of family, race, and neighborhood integrity. It is hard to talk in objective, professional terms about issues of that kind.

It is even harder to talk about the inherent self-correcting immortality of science in a bureaucratic society. The tendencies in either the direction of inhibiting experimentation or encouraging too much experimentation are equally dangerous, and the balance may require more sophistication of management than we now have. More important from my perspective, it may require management capable of transcending the many parochialisms of professional interest and bureaucratic protectionism—and able to tell the difference between the two. That takes insight, a willingness to see a community as a whole, and a sense of the future no professionalism can provide. For centuries uncountable the promise of life after death has been the major source of commitment to the future. We may be on the threshold of having to rely on the future itself for our inspiration.

JOHN McKNIGHT

NEIGHBORHOOD ORGANIZATION, COMMUNITY DEVELOPMENT AND THE ASSUMPTION OF SCARCITY:
The Problem of Equity and Justice

Just over a decade ago, the older neighborhoods of most cities seemed alive with signs of change. There were new federal programs, organizing activities, plans for redevelopment, and people with hope for a new future.

Today, it appears to many observers that the urban neighborhood is nearly dead. They report a sense of powerlessness, expressed in abandoned buildings and charred vacant lots. They note a frustrated anger in the soaring crime rates. And they see a resigned hopelessness in the long lines at the unemployment-compensation office.

If the urban neighborhood was the New Frontier of the 1960s, in 1975 the neighborhood is usually described as a devastated landscape characterized by impotence, anger, and hopelessness. While this popular view is accurate in some respects, it is also misleading because it suggests that the city neighborhood is dying while the rest of the nation is vital and growing. A closer analysis, however, suggests that the sickening symptoms of the urban neighborhood afflict the entire body politic of the country.

Who would say, after all, that most American people are without a sense of powerlessness? Most opinion surveys record a fast-growing sense of general impotence. One recent study, for example, finds that only one in four Americans feels she or he has the power to affect their own future.

Who would say that most American people are not angry? In the aftermath of Vietnam and Watergate, they have been plunged into something called "stagflation." To many people, the country seems to conspire against its own ideals and prospects. They feel betrayed and angry.

Who would say that most American people don't have a sense of hopelessness? The levels of participation in civic, governmental, and electoral activities appear to have diminished recently. We hear many people who were previously active citizens now saying, in resignation, "It won't make any difference."

It is important to recognize, then, that the very same malady that we note in urban neighborhoods is a national disease. It is unlikely, therefore, that we will be able to cure the neighborhood without looking at the problem of the entire body politic.

Perhaps the central fact that best explains the national disease is our belated recognition that there may be limits to growth. We are slowly understanding that we have limited natural resources, limits to the growth of our gross national product, limits to the benefits of technology, and even limits to the service economy. This recognition strikes at the heart of our traditional national assumptions. If the ultimate good is growth, then a society with limits is bad. No wonder many of us, rich, poor, and middle class, feel powerless, angry, and hopeless.

It is very difficult for political leaders to deal with our frustration in the face of limits. They, and we, are used to the politics of distributing more. We are now faced with the untried politics of dividing up less.

There are two critical issues that affect urban neighborhoods as we begin the politics of dividing less.

First, older urban neighborhoods are the homeland of people who have always had less. They are people experienced in dealing with limits. They have developed personal life styles and community networks that enable people to "make do." As a society, it may be that we should learn from the urban ethnic neighborhood how to conserve, rehabilitate, relate, and share. To do this, we may have to forego some of our commitments to growth-oriented planners and managers and reexamine the characteristics of older neighborhoods so that the proper policies for their support can be developed.

Second, as we engage in the politics of limits, the people in urban neighborhoods will be challenged once again to demand basic justice and equity. It was one thing for America to seek justice by distributing its *surplus* to the less advantaged. Programmatically, that form of justice was called the Anti-Poverty Program.

It is a very different thing to seek justice when we have limited resources. And yet, that is what justice is all about. It was never justice in the first place to deal with the disadvantaged by taking more for our-

selves and giving them a piece of the surplus. Justice is the equitable distribution of a limited resource. While our resources have always been limited,
the ideology of growth denied that fact. We substituted surplus for justice.
Now that we perceive the reality of limits, the people in urban neighborhoods are faced with a struggle for a real share of the society rather than
the pieces of its growing edges.

It is clear that the people in urban neighborhoods have had enough
struggle. They don't need more. But it is also clear that they must continue to struggle in order to survive—much less to achieve justice and
equity. This reality is not news to them. It is an old story. Indeed, amid
the prophecies of doomed urban neighborhoods, they have developed
an increasing number of community-based efforts to survive and renew.
Outsiders generally call these efforts self-help groups—a label that may
mean that outsiders don't control, profit by, or understand them.

These groups, their activities and relationships, are not new. They are
indigenous forms of asserting community identity and problem solving.
What is new is the fact that some outsiders—governmental, business, and
academic people—now see them because there is no longer a veil of ex-
ternally imposed programs that masked the basic capacities of neighborhoods to persevere. As these neighborhood self-help efforts continue, it is
important that they be understood in terms of their potential *and* their
limits.

Their potential is related to two facts. First, they express the neighborhood's own problem definitions. Second, they represent the problem-
solving creativity of neighborhood people. In both respects, they differ
from the categorical federal, state, and local programs that define the
problem and the solution from afar. These self-help efforts implicitly
deny the expertise of planners and managers as central to problem defining
and problem solving.

On the other hand, these neighborhood efforts have two critical limits—
the *economic resources* and the *legal authority* to achieve their goals.
These limits are no small matter. But they *are* the limits established and
maintained by the very officials and businessmen who decry the decay
of urban neighborhoods.

The hard fact of the matter is that if we are to enable the capacities of
urban neighborhoods in a society of limits, governmental officials and
business leaders will have radically to revise their assumptions and
practices regarding the economics and authority of urban neighborhoods.
If we do not have the wisdom to undertake the revision, then urban

neighborhood groups must struggle to change our minds. And if they fail, we will all fail.

If we are to alter our course so that we enable the capacities of urban neighborhoods, the revised agenda for governmental leaders requires two major changes:

1. The process of metropolitan growth must now be recognized as a negative factor in a zero-sum game. Every new shopping center, industrial park, and new town on the edge of the city is a use of limited capital that guts the city and hastens urban abandonment. Urban governmental leaders must now use all their powers to insure that any further peripheral growth has a positive tax trade-off for the city—or fight against the development process. A good model for urban politicians is the elected official from rural America. He or she has been a master at trading limited political power for the advantage of rural people—7 percent of our population.

The urban governmental leader must also get tough about using his or her political capacity to stop the flight of job-creating enterprise and investment capital from the city. This is a serious business that requires not only incentives but probably demands restrictive legislation.

2. We must seriously experiment with relocating some of the legal authority of city governments so that local neighborhoods have some of the powers now assigned to city hall. We have widespread evidence that the citizen-participation model of centralized governments has intrinsic limits in producing involvement and responsibility at the neighborhood level. We need something like neighborhood governments if the self-help capacities of neighborhood people are to be effectively developed. This is not to say that all powers should be localized, but the legal power to control basic services and land use may be essential to enabling neighborhood capacity. As the state and city divide their authority for the commonweal, so it is time for the city to divide its authority with the neighborhoods if the city is to survive. Once again, this decision requires us to depend much less upon growth-oriented planners and managers who are trained in ideologies that require centralized systems in order to reach so-called economies of scale.

If the business community is to enable viable urban neighborhoods, at least three basic revisions are necessary:

1. Financial institutions will need to allocate a significant percentage of

their resources for neighborhood and subregional urban development. The problem with this proposal is clear—there is not an adequate return on investment in these neighborhoods. But as we see decreasing demand for capital in the suburban periphery, the new market potential of a society of limits can be the renewal and maintenance of existing neighborhoods and subregions. If this prospect is not developed by the business community, then we can expect more government control of capital flow. Indeed, the current federal and state legislation requiring disclosure of the source of deposits and location of mortgages made by savings and loan institutions may be the precursor of increased regulation over all financial institutions that fail to foresee the importance of conserving neighborhoods.

2. As suburban growth slows, business leaders must recognize that their manpower and markets are no longer at the edge of the city. In a society of limits, they will have to deal with limited manpower pools and markets. So the city and its neighborhoods and schools must be viable, or their future will be limited. Businessmen need productive systems for markets. But if markets are not expanding, then their self-interest is in the redevelopment of market capacity in previously neglected areas—urban neighborhoods.

3. The business community has based much of its growth upon the development of consumer technologies. We have used little of our inventiveness to develop technologies for neighborhood maintenance and development. We have provided people television and gas-eating autos, but we have not developed technologies to maintain urban housing, create cheap solar-energy heating systems or urban systems for food production.

Both business and governmental leaders must also intensify one item on the old agenda if urban neighborhoods are to survive. As a nation, we officially recognized in the 1960s our tragic history of racial exploitation. We enacted laws that could make a difference. Nonetheless, we have begun to ignore them as our limits become obvious. There is no possibility for urban neighborhood renewal in most cities if we revert to institutional racism "as usual." Indeed, the *most* critical issue in maintaining or redeveloping many urban neighborhoods is insuring a just income for minority people. Once again, the critical issue we often face is justice— not planning, programs, or services.

Finally, it may be necessary for the people in urban neighborhoods to consider two questions that have not been readily apparent as they have attempted to help themselves.

First is the lure of services. In many urban neighborhoods, where people are poor, individuals find it difficult to help themselves because they have inadequate incomes. Therefore, they are often sick, ill educated, and unemployed. The traditional response is to provide more services rather than a decent income. Sometimes, neighborhood people see their self-interest as having more services in order to treat their poorness. The ultimate expression of this response is the multiservice center. Understandable as it is, the poor basically need income, not more services. One is not a substitute for the other, unless the poor are *employed* by the service system rather than *treated* by it.

Second, the residents of urban neighborhoods may not recognize the fact that there is the possibility of a new political alliance. The people who live in urban neighborhoods are usually tied to the city. For them, the suburb is not an economic possibility. Because of the developing limits of our economy, there are increasing numbers of middle-class people who are also tied to the city, but tied by their *jobs*. These people include city employees, such as teachers, policemen, and firemen. They now have much less chance to change jobs because the economy isn't growing. But their income is tied to the tax base and general viability of the city. These groups are politically powerful and could soon be important allies in the political struggles to stop the flight of jobs and capital from the city. These groups also have multimillion-dollar pension funds that represent important investment capital which could be used for neighborhood revitalization that could increase the tax base for their own salaries. Indeed, it was the New York City teachers' pension fund that recently bailed out the city because the teachers recognized that their income was related to the city's future.

In summary, we are a society of limits. Our frustrations are not limited to urban neighborhoods. But we are in great danger of killing the city because our governmental and business leaders are so hooked on growth that they can't adjust to the new America of limits. On the other hand, the people in the neighborhoods have lived with limits all their lives. They need leaders who can enable their capacities. Their basic problem may be government and business leaders who aren't prepared to face the new frontier of limits—a frontier that has long been the home of the people who live in urban neighborhoods.

SAM BASS WARNER, Jr.

URBAN DEVELOPMENT AND THE POVERTIES
OF THE NEXT DECADE

This paper considers recent trends in the urban economy and the effects of these trends upon the families living in metropolitan America. Some of the poverties of the future will continue the poverties of the past. They are the products of conditions we have long neglected. Other poverties will be new. They are the products of forces whose mechanisms we are only beginning to recognize and understand. They are the product of the banquet which some Americans have been enjoying since World War II.

My focus will be a typical American metropolis, the recorded and projected experience of Cincinnati from 1950 through 1980. The poverties will be the old ones of the rural fringe and the urban core, and the new ones of the growing service and government economy that is spreading rapidly through the main body of the urban and suburban Cincinnati metropolis.

I will take up each part of the metropolitan region in turn, the fringe, the core, the main body of the metropolis proper (the SMSA), and identify the special properties of each. I will also suggest some remedies appropriate to these parts and to the entire region. In general my understanding of the changing urban economy suggests that the new metropolitan economies of the nation possess the seeds of their own rejuvenation. These seeds lie in the abundance of public goods that urban agglomerations create. At present these seeds are held in the hands of private corporations and are not available for relief of urban poverties. The establishment of public land banks to recapture some of the public value of urban land, and the establishment of public development banks to aid in the public purchase and management of profitable public goods are the major long-run remedies for the current poverty-producing trends in the economy.

The outlines of America's urban development are now clear. Commencing in the 1880s the United States built a nationally integrated economy composed of large industrialized and mechanized metropolises. Millions of farmers abandoned rural America; our rural population declined relatively, and in many places absolutely. The metropolis itself assumed a totally novel urban form—an inner city of business, manufacturing, trade, and slum residence, and an outer city of middle-income and wealthy residence.[1]

For our purposes it is sufficient to note one peculiarity of this earlier era. Although the poverties of the years since 1880 were more rural than urban, and although the new nationally integrated economy contained the possibility, if not the willingness, for national planning to deal with these poverties, no national response from the federal government was forthcoming. It was a peculiarity of this era, and a peculiarity of the New Deal, Fair Deal, and Great Society years since then, that local governments have been the only active American planning agents. Thus, whether local governments have been nasty and defensive, or well-intentioned and open—and they have been both—they were coping with poverties whose networks of cause and effect lay far beyond the reach of their several jurisdictions.

Since perhaps 1929, certainly since World War II, urban America has been moving in new directions. Because of interregional migration, specialization in agriculture, private economic investment, and government spending, the great disparities in personal income among the metropolitan regions of the nation have leveled up. In 1929 metropolitan New York's per-capita personal income was six times that of the poorest region in the United States (Florence, S.C.). It now stands at only two-and-a-half times that of the poorest region (Brownsville, Texas). In 1929 Cincinnati's per-capita personal income exceeded the national average by 25 percent; it now is, and is projected to remain, at the mean level.[2] This trend toward intermetropolitan parity cannot be said to have been the product of national debate and conscious planning policy in the past. The subject, however, must become such if we are to plan for a more equitable economy in the future.

During these same years the metropolis itself assumed yet another form. The single dominant downtown center gave way to a pattern of many centers of industry, retailing, wholesaling, offices, and professional services. The old downtown, shorn of much of its manufacturing, wholesaling, and retailing, became one among many business concentrations. This outmigration of employment paralleled, perhaps even encouraged, the further spread of residential suburbs so that the core-city slums expanded in area, although like the rest of the metropolis, they fell in density. In addition, improved national transportation and communications accelerated the growth of large corporate marketing and production firms, so that private capital came to dominate the success or failure of suburban shopping centers and industrial parks. Indeed, now that large private corporations are moving directly into land speculation and development, the power imbalance between a local-government planning agency and those it seeks to guide and control becomes every year more severe.

Three less discussed changes of the post-World War II era also must be attended to. First, the United States and its metropolitan economies possess a very different structure than they did thirty years ago. Many Americans now make their living in new ways. Agriculture, mining, manufacturing, transportation, communications and public utilities, wholesaling and retailing, have been declining relatively as a source of earnings for the nation's employees. The growing sectors of the economy from 1950 through 1980 are finance, insurance, and real estate, up 48.7 percent; services, up 59.8 percent; and government, up 53.0 percent. Especially state-and local-government employment earnings are up, 103.6 percent for the thirty year period (Table 1). Contract construction showed a slight growth until the recent depression.[3] Unfortunately, only government, in the earnings growth list, represents well-paid, secure jobs for most of its participants (Table 2). It is in this shift in the structure of the economy that the new poverties are to be found.

Second, since World War II the federal government has become a major factor in determining regional growth. The cause is not direct federal employment, but the federal influence lies in the differential effects of its taxation and expenditures. Thus, not only does the newly integrated, metropolitan private economy suggest the possibility of planning, but also the actual government allocations of national resources function as central plans without conferring any of the benefits of conscious planning and openly debated decisions.

The nature of federal taxes and the objects and location of federal spending are not crucial issues for every metropolis in the country. For example, the Cincinnati metropolis encompasses parts of three states: Ohio, Indiana, and Kentucky. A recent study shows that these three states, on a yearly average, paid to the federal government $3.8 billion more than they received in federal disbursements of all kinds. In planning terms, $3.8 billion per year would be an enormous development budget for these three states. Indeed, the sum is of the magnitude of New York City's request for bond guarantees! At the same time California showed a net gain from the federal government of $2.1 billion, and New York State a net loss of $7.5 billion.[4] Surely the nature and source of federal taxation and disbursements and their regional effects upon economic development must become the subjects for political debate and conscious management.

TABLE 1

Changes in the Economic Structure of the United States and the Cincinnati BEA, 1950-1980

SECTOR	PERCENTAGE OF TOTAL EARNINGS					
	United States			Cincinnati BEA		
	1950	1969/70	1980	1950	1969/70	1980
Agriculture, forestry, fishing	9.1	3.7	2.5	6.1	2.1	1.2
Mining	2.0	1.0	0.8	0.2	0.2	0.1
Contract Construction	6.0	6.2	6.2	5.3	6.8	6.3
Manufactures	28.9	28.6	26.2	38.7	37.9	34.7
Transportation, communication, public utilities	8.2	6.9	7.0	8.8	7.2	7.4
Wholesale and retail trade	18.9	16.1	16.0	19.2	16.5	15.9
Finance, insurance, real estate	3.9	5.2	5.8	4.1	4.6	5.3
Services	11.2	14.7	17.9	10.6	13.2	16.5
Government	11.5	16.9	17.6	6.9	11.3	12.4
federal	(3.7)	(4.3)	(4.3)	(1.8)	(2.6)	(2.6)
state and local	(5.6)	(9.8)	(11.4)	(4.7)	(8.2)	(9.5)
federal military	(2.2)	(2.8)	(1.9)	(0.4)	(0.5)	(0.3)

Source: U.S.D.C., Bureau of Economic Analysis, *Area Economic Projections 1990*

Third, and finally, the possibilities of the new wealth created by the increased urbanization of the nation should be understood. As more and more of the nation comes to live in urban agglomerations, the economic returns to large-scale activities increase. We are familiar with the historical accumulation of new technology which made large-scale production of such complicated products as automobiles possible. At the same time we fail to notice that the rise of metropolitan markets has brought a parallel reduction in the cost of marketing and servicing products like automobiles. The new returns to scale are not just situated in factories; as importantly, they reside in the metropolis. Machines, for instance, do not explain all the causes for the replacement of the corner grocer by the supermarket, or the rise of nationally owned metropolitan brewing chains. The consequence of increasing technological skill and increasing urbanization has been an ever-lengthening list of goods and services that are the universal consumption items of our society.

TABLE 2

U.S. Annual Earnings per Employee by Industrial Sector 1969/1970

Sector of Employees	Number of Employees	Earnings per Employee
Agriculture, forestry, fishing	2,840,488	$ 7,071
Mining	630,788	8,589
Contract Construction	4,572,215	7,515
Manufactures	19,837,208	8,155
Transportation, communication, public utilities	5,186,101	7,455
Wholesale and retail trade	15,372,880	5,948
Finance, insurance, real estate	3,838,387	7,523
Services	15,750,836	5,206
Government	8,524,676	11,025
Total Employed	76,553,599	7,270

Source: *1970 U.S. Census of Population: Characteristics of the Population*, vol. 1, pt. 1 (U.S. Summary), table 92; U.S.D.C., *Area Economic Projections 1990*

Today's trends go back at least to the twenties, and the list of goods and services transformed far exceeds the home appliances and automotive products that most readily come to mind. The group of universal goods and services that show strong economies of scale include such items as food products and drugs, health care, secondary and higher education, and the provision of recreation. Housing will soon join the group. In these goods and services lie the new profits and new wealth of the society. The way they are now produced and provided causes the poverties of our metropolitan era. Their wealth, however, if judiciously harnessed to public purposes, could be the source of an ample economic and social justice.

In terms of poverties these historical changes in the metropolitanization of our society and its economy have meant that large numbers of urban Americans live at below the average level of both public and private goods and services. To be poor at the center of the metropolis now means lower-than-average wages and higher-than-average uncertainty of employment. It also means higher prices in the local stores, and no way to purchase many of the universal goods of the society: lower health, education, and other publicly provided services, and a higher fraction of the family budget paid out in rents, and often in taxes as well. To be poor on the fringe is to suffer similar conditions. Taxes and housing may be less expensive on the fringe, but low-quality housing and often low-quality or nonexistent public services cancel out any superficial savings. Put another way, the poor of America's metropolises disproportionately bear the costs of urbanization without reaping equivalent benefits.

The case of Cincinnati nicely illustrates these historical trends. A three-state, twenty-eight-county, metropolitan commuting and shopping region of about 2,000,000 inhabitants, its old and new poverties can be easily identified by splitting the region into three parts: the fringe of 501,198 inhabitants, the metropolis proper of 1,240,595, and the poverty core of 136,000.[5]

THE FRINGE

The outer fringes of American metropolitan regions are not acting out ceaseless success stories of land boom, growth, and prosperity. Neither is the fringe of Cincinnati. The outer Cincinnati counties in Ohio, Indiana, and Kentucky are characterized by heavy outmigration of their population, modest net-population growth, low earnings per employee, and low per-capita income. In 1950 average earnings on the fringe were but 72.2 percent of the average of the employees in the metropolis proper (the SMSA); in 1980 they are estimated to climb a bit to 78.2 percent of the SMSA, still a very substantial gap since the cost of living is not less in the country than the city.[6]

Such gains as the fringe has made came from growth in four relatively high wage sectors of the American economy—construction; transportation; finance and real estate; and government. Above all, the gains came from government. The fringe was already in 1950 more dependent upon state and local government for its earnings than the Cincinnati SMSA, and the projected growth to 1980 is for a 142 percent increase (Tables 2, 3, and 5).

The other special characteristic of the fringe has been the rapid decline in agricultural earnings (70.4 percent, 1950-1980), but the area continues to rely substantially on agriculture as a source of employment and family income (Table 3).

TABLE 3

Changes in the Economic Structure of the Cincinnati Fringe, 1950-1980
Sector Earnings as a Percentage of Total Earnings

| | PERCENTAGE OF TOTAL EARNINGS | | |
	1950	1969/1970	1980
Agriculture, forestry, fishing	21.3	8.3	5.3
Mining	0.1	0.1	0.1
Contract Construction	4.2	7.4	7.6
Manufactures	39.5	40.0	37.1
Transportation, communication, public utilities	3.5	3.7	4.2
Wholesale and retail trade	14.4	13.5	13.2
Finance, insurance, real estate	2.3	2.9	3.7
Services	7.0	9.7	12.5
Government	7.7	14.4	16.5
federal	(1.0)	(1.7)	(1.3)
state and local	(6.2)	(11.8)	(15.0)
federal military	(0.5)	(0.9)	(0.2)

Note: The Cincinnati fringe is made up of those counties in the Cincinnati BEA which were not part of the Cincinnati SMSA, namely: Adams, Brown, Butler, Clinton, and Highland in Ohio; Fayette, Franklin, Ohio, Ripley, Switzerland, and Union in Indiana; and Bracken, Carroll, Fleming, in Kentucky.
Source: U.S.D.C. Bureau of Economic Analysis, *Area Economic Projections 1990,* values established by subtracting Cincinnati SMSA data from Cincinnati BEA data

Such a brief summary of the changing structure of the economy of a metropolitan fringe suggests several important points about the poverties of the future.

First, the old inequalities of the distribution of national wealth between rural and urban America persist. The past policies of the U.S. Department of Agriculture and its related-interest groups have been unable or unwilling to deal with this long-standing inequality. Thus for many reasons, as people concerned with an equitable distribution of American wealth, as receivers of those driven off the land, as consumers of agricultural products, and as the ultimate developers of much agricultural land, the metropolises of the United States have a deep interest in conditions on the fringe. Strange as it may sound to urban ears, metropolitan America must develop an agricultural policy for the nation as a whole, and within each region it must create and carry out fringe employment and development plans.

Second, the new economy appears dramatically in the fringe. In particular, it appears in its extraordinary dependence on government for its employment earnings. By 1980 government-employment earnings will be three times those of agriculture and second only to manufacturing as a source of income for fringe residents. As in the case of the nation's metropolises, whose growth now strongly depends upon the taxes and allocations of the federal government, here again we encounter unplanned public spending as a major support of a population's well-being.

The spread of the metropolis outward, especially in the form of construction and manufacturing, is the source of the fringe's private gains. In this case, the public-private power imbalances are extreme and probably bear disproportionately upon the fringe low-income residents. Currently fringe areas in the United States give tax concessions, and often develop land and even put up buildings for manufacturers who will locate in the area. Competition exists among such areas, and manufacturers can bargain among them for the best concessions, the largest site subsidy. The goal of the fringe is to seek long-run prosperity by attracting industry, but the costs in many cases may well exceed the local gains. Even modest concessions hurt most residents not employed at the new plant, since the public costs are spread through the population by a regressive tax system. In short, as things presently stand, the poor on the fringe must subsidize most of their own economic development.

Under these circumstances if the fringe by itself, or even better, in conjunction with the metropolitan region, would engage in land banking and public-development banking—that is, holding vacant land and selling it for public profit to commercial and residential purchasers, and operating public banks to lend money to desirable public and private firms—the poor taxpayers would reap some of the development profits, not just absorb the costs. Public land and public-development banking are both promising remedies for the lagging fringe and core economies; they are also highly desirable for the income problems of the metropolis proper.[7]

TABLE 4

Employment Structure of the Cincinnati Inner-City Core, 1970

SECTOR	EMPLOYED			
	Male	Females	Total	Percentage
Agriculture, forestry, fishing	66	0	66	0.1
Mining	0	0	0	0.0
Contract Construction	2,186	60	2,246	4.7
Manufactures	9,329	3,394	12,723	26.7
Transportation, communications, public utilities	1,881	664	2,545	5.3
Wholesale and retail trade	3,915	3,048	6,963	14.6
Finance, insurance, real estate	590	819	1,409	3.0
Services	4,037	9,562	13,599	28.6
Government	4,405	3,616	8,021	16.9
Total	26,409	21,163	47,572	99.9

Source: U.S. Census, *Employment Profiles of Selected Low-Income Areas, Cincinnati,* Table 11

THE CORE

The center-city slum has been a topic for journalists and social investigators for at least a century now, yet its poverties are generally misrepresented in this literature, and effective public action has yet to be taken. As its contribution to the late War on Poverty, the U.S. Bureau of the Census conducted a special canvass of sixty-eight inner-city low-income areas. The great merit of this recent study is that it clearly demonstrates that the problem of the core, as of the fringe, is not lounging teen-age boys, or pregnant girls, but low wages, uncertain jobs, and high unemployment and underemployment. The major problems of the core are the problems of the working poor and the effects that the metropolitan economy has upon their family life.

In Cincinnati the area chosen by the census was the Mill Creek, inner-city, and river neighborhoods. The study portrays the social and economic circumstances of 136,000 members of the metropolis: 58 percent were Negro; 42 percent were white.[8] As throughout the metropolis, the nature of an area's structure is crucial to its well-being. Here at the core the employment structure (Table 4) has two peculiarities. First, core workers are underrepresented in earnings from manufacturing, transportation, communications and utilities, finance, insurance and real estate, wholesale and retail trade. Instead they are heavily concentrated in services—a low wage sector of the economy. Second, the historical path of government employment as the source of secure, well-paid jobs appears in today's Cincinnati core, as it did in the days of the immigrant political machines. Twice the proportion of core employees are working for government as in the metropolis proper (core, 16.9 percent; SMSA 8.5 percent, 1970).

Despite this governmental opportunity, overall employee earnings are low, similar to those on the fringe, in this case 70.8 percent; of the SMSA (core, $5,402; fringe, $6,002; SMSA, $7,626, 1970). Most core-city jobs pay low wages, are uncertain, and despite efforts of the residents to find jobs, unemployment is high. Thus, the overall labor-force participation rate in the core is below the national and the regional level (55.7 percent vs. national 60.3 percent), and unemployment is especially severe in the teen years (in 1970 it stood at 25.7 percent).[9]

The consequences that follow from this kind of economy tell a very old story. The recent excellent studies like Carol B. Stack's *All Our Kin* (1974) or Elliot Liebow's *Tally's Corner* (1967) repeat the reports of Charles Booth's London of the 1890s. Low wages and unemployment destroy families, and drive women involuntarily into the labor market where they meet more low wages, and a further cycle of social and economic harassment. The median income of Cincinnati's core families in 1970 was $5,950; the median size of families, 3.7. The then current Bureau of Labor Statistics minimum budget for an urban family of four stood at $6,960.[10] The failure of many of the men and women of the core to be able, either singly or together, to earn a decent family living destroys their families. In 1970, 27.5 percent of the core's families were female-headed (7 percent, white; 20.5 percent, black). Black women worked in greater proportion than their white sisters (47.5 percent vs. 39.7 percent), and all these female-headed households suffered extreme impoverishment (average per family income, female head: white, $3,481; black, $3,119).[11]

In simplest summary terms, the core—like the fringe—is disproportionately absorbing the costs of the unemployment, lay-offs, and low
wages of the metropolitan economy. Its residents are the direct victims of
the callousness of the modes of the American economy. To receive justice
immediately the core, like the fringe, needs higher national minimum
wages, full employment, and a guaranteed opportunity to do useful work
through the government serving as an employer of last resort. In the long
run, public-development strategies and public ownership of the profitable
universal goods of the metropolis will be the best way to secure the well-
being of core families. Such strategies are also the best hope for the
families of the metropolis proper who face the new poverties of the future.

THE PRINCIPAL METROPOLIS (SMSA)

The trends of the future for metropolitan poverty can best be understood by following the predicament of an average Cincinnati family. In
1970 the average earnings of Cincinnati employees were $7,626. That
year such an income for a family of four in which only the husband
worked and supported a wife and two children fell $1,000 above the
Department of Labor's minimum budget. Taxes and social security would
take 16 percent off the earnings and what remained was used to find a
five-room rental unit and purchase a six-year-old car once every four
years, leaving $700 a year for all the extras of family life. Thirty-four
percent of the nation's families whose wives did not work were in a
comparable situation.

For many families, however, the consequences of such a budget squeeze
has been to send the wife out to seek work. Again at the national level,
from 1950 to 1970 female participation in the labor force has risen to
42.6 percent of all women sixteen years old and over. The most dramatic
shift, however, has been among that group of married women who have
children and husbands who live with them. Their participation rate has
jumped from 28.3 percent in 1950 to 49.2 percent in 1970.[12]

Before we consider whether this is a new opportunity or a new burden
for metropolitan America, let us look at shifts in the structure of the
economy which faced Cincinnati's families (Table 5). The structural
trend has set strongly toward the low-wage sectors of the economy. The
share of employee earnings declined, and is projected to decline, in manufacturing; transportation, communications, public utilities; wholesale

and retail trade. The shift is towards finance, insurance, and real estate; services; and government (finance, up 26.1 percent; services, up 50.4 percent; government, up 71.2 percent). The relative losses in high-wage unionized manufacturing and in transportation, communications, and public utilities have not been recaptured in equivalent gains in finance, insurance, and real estate or in government. Instead the big growth category has been in services—health, entertainment, restaurants, business and professional services—which as a group of activities pay the lowest wages in the metropolis except for the minor agricultural and mining sectors. The earnings level in services is about one-third below the Cincinnati metropolitan level (70.1 percent of $7,626, 1970 SMSA). Thus as wives and mothers leave the home, they meet opportunities most frequently in low-wage, nonunionized services, or often in retailing, the next worst-paying sector.[13]

Herein lie the ingredients for the new metropolitan poverties. Families unable to keep up with inflation, wives working full-time, women and wives working at low-wage jobs; women and machines being substituted for men; unemployment payments rising as the labor-market participants grow in numbers because more people attempt to participate in the labor force; taxes rising to take up the slack in the private economy, to offer public services that formerly were offered through the home and the neighborhood; inflation caused by armaments and fiscal attempts to deal with unemployment. There is nothing in either the recent national or Cincinnati data to suggest that if no public remedies are undertaken these costly trends will not continue. If we do nothing, the fringe and the core will continue to fail to catch up with the metropolis proper; the principal metropolis will experience impoverishment of many of its working-class and lower-middle-class families and neighborhoods. In local terms, the future suggests a good deal of housing deterioration, public-service declines, and a general fall in the quality of life in Cincinnati, both city and suburbs.

Let me conclude, not by elaborating on the ramifications of family-income loss as it strikes an urban community, but by suggesting an approach to wages, employment, and the metropolitan and national economies that would both end the injustices of the present poverties, and also improve the quality of life for all residents of the city.

First, the changing nature of Cincinnati's economy, both the locational and structural elements, attest to the necessity of a more humane wages policy. No one should have to work for less than living wages. As a beginning,

I would define a living wage to be that rate that would enable any adult to support another adult and one child by full-time work, at the Department of Labor's minimum budget (adjusted for inflation). Such a wage would allow single women to support their children, allow married women to choose to stay home if they wished, even allow a married man to stay home if his wife worked. America is not a slave-labor camp; the two-income family should be a matter of choice.

TABLE 5

Changes in the Economic Structure of the Cincinnati SMSA, 1950-1980 Sector Earnings as a Percentage of Total Earnings

	PERCENTAGE TOTAL EARNINGS		
	1950	1969/1970	1980
Agriculture, forestry, fishing	1.8	0.4	0.1
Mining	0.2	0.1	0.1
Contract Construction	5.6	6.6	5.9
Manufactures	38.5	37.3	34.1
Transportation, communication, public utilities	10.4	8.2	8.3
Wholesale and retail trade	20.6	17.5	16.7
Finance, insurance, real estate	4.6	5.1	5.8
Services	11.7	14.2	17.6
Government	6.6	10.4	11.3
federal	(2.0)	(2.9)	(3.0)
State and local	(4.2)	(7.3)	(7.9)
federal military	(0.4)	(0.2)	(0.4)

Source: U.S.D.C., Bureau of Economic Analysis, *Area-Economic Projections 1990*

Second, underemployment and unemployment are surely terrible curses, a visiting of products of economic greed and mismanagement upon those least able to defend themselves. Every adult American who presents himself or herself for work should be able to get a job. Given the mess we are in at the moment, such a policy will require for a time very heavy government employment.

Third, inflation and the rapid increase of especially federal military and state and local governmental activities that do not earn a return on their capital are rapidly eating up all the real-income gains of the society. "Stagflation" is the fashionable word used to describe this trend. The immediate antidote consists of more accountability for governmental activities, drastic cuts in defense expenditures, and federal tax reform and tax equalization among the classes of the population and among the metropolitan regions of the nation. Such reforms will ease the present crisis, but will not in the long run make the nation's economy more productive, so that all Americans can have decent wages and certain employment. The long-run answer to the trends since 1950 lie in national, regional, and local development-planning strategies that take advantage of the special features of our metropolitan economies. Our goal must be to lower costs and raise wages for ordinary American families.

Recall for the minute that in the historical development of our urban economies since World War II, we have arrived at a state where large numbers of goods and services are universally consumed, or almost universally consumed. Many of these goods and services offer substantial returns to large-scale production and marketing. Here is where public development should be concentrated. Federal and state development banks should finance the public ownership and management of the most profitable of such goods and services. By so doing, the public will get a return on its capital investment, and through savings in production and marketing, the gains can be used either to raise wages for low-income workers, as in the case of most services, food processing, and the like; or to reduce costs to all families as in the case of utilities, automobiles, major appliances, and housing.

The moral basis for public ownership of such activities lies in the fact that these universal or near universal goods and services are themselves products of the urbanization of us all. They have been hastened into being by our habit of living in metropolitan clusters. Just as the society creates the value of urban land, so too it creates much of the value of its universal goods. Contrast, if you will, the business possibilities of the electric utility or auto dealer, or appliance salesman, in rural Montana with the position of his opposite in Cincinnati. The altered profitability lies in the clustering of the population, not in the energy or wit of the salesman.

The most promising areas for public ownership, either on the federal or state level, are those in which a single large private corporation or a few large ones now control the product lines. The very presence of such large businesses is a significant clue that the metropolitan markets of the nation have created substantial profit margins in those products. Since such products do not require great variety and elaboration—they are universal goods—the profits from such businesses can be socialized without any loss of innovation or productivity in the society.

In sum, the history of the United States clearly reveals the sequence of development toward today's nation of metropolitan economies. Because the public wealth generated by these metropolitan clusters has been largely siphoned off to private corporations and reinvested in products and services for the middle and upper-income populations, these economies inevitably produce their own poverties. It is an unfortunate fact of our history that the movement toward public planning was bottled up in local government and narrowed to concerns of real-estate development and municipal investment. These are important concerns, to be sure, but with the national and metropolitan economies not planned or managed for public benefit, the mayor, the city manager, the city planner, the social worker, the schoolteacher, the doctor and the nurse, have been left with the ceaseless task of nursing the victims of state capitalism.

After forty years of New Deals, Urban Renewals, and Great Societies, all manner of goodwill, local initiative, conflict, and public effort within the framework of government aid to business, it is time that we recognized that every urban fringe, suburb, city, and core slum in the nation has a common need to capture the value that our metropolitan life creates. Let us not make the mistake that the early socialists of Europe did when they used the government to pick up the faltering parts of their capitalist economies—the railroads and coal mines; let us instead concentrate on the public development of universal goods that will return the greatest profits and cost savings. Only in this way can we deal equitably with the old and new poverties of the nation.

NOTES

1. Zane L. Miller, *The Urbanization of Modern America, A Brief History* (New York, 1973); Sam Bass Warner, Jr., *The Urban Wilderness, A History of the American City* (New York, 1972), Pt. II.

2. For the purposes of this paper the Cincinnati region is the tristate—Ohio, Indiana, Kentucky—twenty-eight-county area which has been identified and defined by the U.S. Department of Commerce as Bureau of Economic Analysis Area (BEA) # 062. It is a unified labor market and retail region. For the rationale behind this regional system of accounts see U.S. Department of Commerce, Regional Economic

Analysis Division, "The BEA Economic Areas: Structural Change and Growth, 1950-73," *Survey of Current Business*, 55 (November 1975), pp. 14-25. The income reports and estimates for the region, the SMSA, and the fringe, and most national data come from U.S.D.C., Bureau of Economic Analysis, *Area Economic Projections 1990* (Washington, n.d. [October 1974]), and same author, *OBERS Projections*, 1 (Washington, 1972).

3. Percent change by sector calculated from the data in Table 1.

4. All figures from James R. Anderson, "The Balance of Military Payments among States and Regions," in Seymour Melman, *The War Economy of the United States* (New York, 1971), pp. 137-47.

5. The population of the Cincinnati BEA in 1970 was 1,902,963; the fringe population was 501,198 (BEA population minus SMSA population); the population of the core was 136,000; the population of the metropolis proper was 1,240,595 (SMSA population minus the core population). Where possible the metropolis proper has been defined by subtracting the core data from the SMSA, but in some cases this was not possible, and the entire SMSA had to be used as the measure for conditions in the metropolis proper.

6. Fringe population growth, 1950-1980, is expected to be 35.5 percent as opposed to the SMSA growth of 46.1 percent. The earnings per employee in 1950 were $3,752; in 1980 they are expected to be $7,368; per capita income in 1950, $1,642; in 1980, $4,208. All data are in constant 1967 dollars. U.S.D.C., Bureau of Economic Analysis, *Area Economic Projections 1990*.

7. Bennett Harrison, *Urban Economic Development* (Washington, 1974).

8. U.S. Bureau of the Census, *Census of Population. 1970, Employment Profiles of Selected Low Income Areas*, PHC (3) 37, *Cincinnati* (Washington, 1972).

9. National data, U.S.B.C., *Statistical Abstract of the United States: 1971* (Washington, 1971), Table 328; Cincinnati SMSA, *Census of Population: 1970, General Social and Economic Characteristics, Ohio, pt. 1* (Washington, 1973), Table 87; Cincinnati Core, *Employment Profiles, Cincinnati*, Tables I, 1, and 24.

10. U.S. Department of Labor, Bureau of Labor Statistics, *Three Budgets for an Urban Family of Four Persons 1969-70. Supplement to Bulletin #15705* (Washington, 1972).

11. *Employment Profiles, Cincinnati*, Tables B, I, and 1.

12. *Statistical Abstract:* 1971, Table 332, 333.

13. *Census of Population: 1970, Ohio Pt. 1*, Table 87.

PART TWO

THE UNFINISHED AGENDA:
Housing and the Question of Race

THE EDITORS

OVERVIEW AND PREVIEW

The contemporary metropolitan crisis suggests not only that we respond imaginatively to new trends and directions in the urbanization process but also that we think in new ways about old problems. In a sense, of course, all our current difficulties are legacies of the past, pressing problems for which past solutions proved inadequate, that past generations simply ignored, or that past generations saw not as problems but as inevitable and "natural" consequences of the human condition. Among these, none is more pressing today than housing and the persistence of the black ghetto, two issues addressed by Jacob B. Ward and Richard C. Wade in the following essays and two issues inextricably intertwined since the late nineteenth century.

Beginning with the advent of the horse-drawn street railway and the short-run steam railroad in the mid-nineteenth century, and proceeding through the adoption of the electric trolley after 1885 and the development and popularization of the auto, truck, and bus in the early twentieth century, technologically improved modes of mass rapid transit laid the foundation for the "step-up" theory of housing. These new means of travel enlarged dramatically the arena of urban life, separating workplace from home and making ever-broadening geographic areas available for residential subdivision. With that, the chance to get a better dwelling in a better neighborhood became the great reward for doing what society asked. For most metropolitanites, securing an education, getting a job, and building a family served as a preface not so much for upward occupational as for outward residential mobility, and the classic pattern took immigrants, newcomers, and their children from the worst central-city slums "up" and out into better areas until they reached greener neighborhoods vacated by similarly mobile lower-middle and middle-class families, while more affluent residents pushed the suburban frontier ever outward in a receding circumference from the central business district, expanding inner-city slums and working and white-collar outer-city neighborhoods.

Into the 1920s the private sector of the economy carried the burden of providing a housing stock sufficient for the minimal needs of the burgeoning and sprawling metropolitan population, and the pressure of the demand almost invariably exceeded the flexibility of the supply of decent housing units, especially in the poor, lower and lower-middle-class districts. Indeed, by the late nineteenth-century, housing had been identified as an important municipal problem, and from that date forward, citizens charged city officials with the responsibility for improving housing conditions. Tenements attracted the bulk of the initial interest, and the first response centered on establishing and enforcing building codes providing minimum standards of light, ventilation, sanitation, and fire safety for new buildings and in the maintenance of the older housing stock. By the early decades of the twentieth-century, as housing reformers began to think in neighborhood and land-use terms, they sought to protect residential areas from commercial and industrial encroachment and "blight" through the legal device of zoning. But the housing problem always seemed to outrun municipal resources, and beginning in the 1920s, as Jacob B. Ward points out, state authorities supplemented city regulation and maintenance efforts by offering various financial subsidies to private interests to stimulate new construction, a program adopted by the federal government in the 1930s and pursued since that time in a series of federal schemes to promote the public and private development of middle-income as well as of low and moderate-income, housing.

Though these policies scarcely made residential Utopias out of American cities, they worked sufficiently well so that the realities of the housing market approximated expectations in a fit close enough to support the credibility of the step-up theory. Metropolitan sprawl persisted through the 1920s, stalled during the depression and World War II, but resumed in the prosperity of the 1950s and 1960s. The functioning of the step-up process since the late nineteenth-century, moreover, contributed to the dilution of compact settlements of immigrant groups, whose members gradually filtered out of concentrated "ethnic" neighborhoods and dispersed across the face of the metropolis in successively less-concentrated agglomerations. Yet the step-up process proved partial. As Richard C. Wade points out, it served whites only. Black neighborhoods expanded contiguously, maintaining their "ethnic" integrity, preserving in expanded form the solid black ghetto that first took shape in the late nineteenth century, and compounding the late twentieth century housing problem with the vexing and explosive question of racial segregation.

As we enter the last quarter of the twentieth-century, both the familiar housing policies of building codes, zoning, and subsidy and the racially skewed step-up theory seem bankrupt. Inflation and mushrooming construction costs now jeopardize both the step-up process and the public policies that buttressed it, confronting us with a housing shortage whose dimensions and context defy conventional wisdom and whose social and political consequences grow daily more grim under the rising pressure generated by the persistence of racial segregation in housing. While some ignore half the problem and others throw up their hands in despair, Wade and Ward challenge us to think about this dual problem. Both, moreover, either implicitly or explicitly, call into question the ability of this generation of urban professionals to handle the question. Wade contends that planners here and abroad have failed both to understand and to control the urbanization process, then proposes a policy to remove race as a divisive and distracting factor in our efforts to meet the housing problem. Ward, on the other hand, though a self-styled optimist, analyzes past efforts to subsidize low and moderate-income housing and concludes pessimistically that policy makers seem unable even to ask the hard questions about how to meet a housing shortage which now, as in the past, hits the poor and moderate-income individuals hardest and increasingly infringes upon the traditional aspirations of the middle classes as well. Together, the two essays dramatize the need and establish a framework for new ways of thinking about the historical legacy and current configuration of the issues of housing and race in metropolitan America, which threaten to disrupt the fabric of society and jeopardize the future peace of the metropolis.

JACOB B. WARD

METROPOLITAN HOUSING:
The Closing Frontier

Scarcely ten years ago, the late Charles Abrams completed his study on urban renewal in the United States. He entitled it *The City Is the Frontier*, and in its opening pages he declared, "In our own era, the world cities are witnessing their greatest surge in man's history; everywhere hoards of people are leaving the hinterlands in search of the cities' opportunities, its excitement and its way of life. From 1800 to 1950 the proportion of people living in cities with more than 20,000 leaped from 2.4 percent to 21 percent. This advance into the cities is one of the spectacular social phenomena of our times. The city has become the frontier."[1]

What happened in ten short years? Is the urban frontier now in danger of becoming a gigantic ghost town? Is my title too pessimistic? Why do I believe, at least with respect to housing in metropolitan areas, that the frontier is rapidly coming to a close, that opportunities are ending?

First, I am an attorney, and law and its pursuit as a profession provide a particular training, a mode of thinking, a way of conceptualizing. Plato had inscribed over the doorway of his academy, "Let no man enter here who does not know geometry," for he believed that the man who could not handle the relatively simple abstractions of mathematics would certainly be unable to handle the more complex abstractions of law and justice. Or to paraphrase in a way more appropriate to this occasion, one must be willing to come to grips with a multitude of complex abstractions to comprehend the complexity of housing in the metropolis, which involves questions of law, politics, economics, and justice, among others. It is also important, I think, that one should approach the issue of housing in the metropolis as a disinterested inquirer—disinterested in the same sense that a judge trying a case must remain disinterested.

The posture of disinterest, however, is difficult for me to maintain because I worked in government for almost seventeen years and during practically all those years I worked in the field of housing. With respect to the early and middle years of my government service, it might be said I had a disinterested view of housing, for my basic duties then involved the defense of court challenges to state and city actions, and I got paid at the end of the week or month whether I won or lost. During the latter part of my career in government, however, I became an administrator and assumed the protective coloration indigenous to that breed. In those years I became involved with certain experimental housing rehabilitation programs in the belief that they might, in some small way, assist in alleviating what seems to be a chronic housing problem in New York City. These undertakings were by no means unqualified successes. One might say that their value sometimes consisted as much in establishing what could not be done as in demonstrating what could be achieved. Indeed, because we are in large measure a success-oriented culture, we might be kind and describe some of these endeavors as pedagogical successes rather than projects that provided shelter and reasonable rents.

I left government more than ten years ago, and in these last ten years either as an attorney, consultant, packager, or as a developer, I have been involved in the development of new housing and in the rehabilitation of existing housing in a score of cities. I have been involved with housing developments as large as several thousand units and as small as seven. In the main, most of my endeavors have been in the area of new housing construction involving governmental assistance programs.

Altogether, then, I have roughly thirty years of housing experience of one kind or another, and it is that experience which has led me to my current pessimistic outlook on the topic. It has convinced me that for thirty years the housing stock in most of our older central cities has been deteriorating. That stock desperately requires renovation and renewal. Worse still, over that thirty-year period the supply of new housing consistently fell short of the real need. Finally, that experience has convinced me that providing good and adequate housing is an important factor in assuring the viability of the future of the metropolis.

Housing is clearly a most important segment of any metropolis, and it is an extraordinarily complicated subject. Indeed, any aspect of the diverse elements relating to the existence of the metropolis, such as transportation patterns, educational or health facilities, of necessity has an important effect on existing housing as well as upon the potential for new housing. John Donne's statement about no man being an island may easily be transposed with respect to housing in the metropolis. While conceding this point, however, we need to pay particular attention to housing as a discrete problem if for no other reason than because it is so costly. It is probably the single most expensive purchase made by most families, and most families devote a substantial part of their budgets either to paying off the purchase of their homes or to paying the rent on their dwellings. It is, in the jargon of the economy, a capital-intensive commodity.

Housing is also important because it may be a significant contributing factor to many social ills. Poor health, low levels of educational achievement, and high crime rates are often cited as resulting from bad housing. And if a direct causal relationship among these factors has never been adequately established in the view of some, their coincidence is too prevalent not to warrant governmental intervention in the view of many. Beyond that, moreover, bad housing not only affects the particular owner or tenant but also his neighbors and the neighborhood. Bad housing drives out good housing, and upon such a rationale many recognize the need for and encourage public action. For all these reasons, public action taken by many states and municipalities with respect to housing involved an attempt to prevent or eliminate slums and provide an adequate supply of decent safe and sanitary housing by enacting building codes for minimum standards of light and air, room size, and sanitary facilities. At the same time, we can and have passed statutes that impose maintenance and service standards designed to prevent good housing from becoming bad. But is is clear that while such legislation provides standards, it does not produce new housing. It simply prevents the new housing being built from being bad housing or, where successful, prevents existing housing from going bad.

Yet housing, no matter how long lasting, either deteriorates or is lost for one reason or another from the inventory; and population growth, no matter how much it is slowed, nevertheless does result in new family formations, new styles of living, and new demands upon the housing stock. Worse still, the market forces to correct shortages or deficiencies in housing take so long that by the time you meet the deficiency that existed three years ago you have a new problem. Because of this fact, among others, we in this country have recognized that housing is sufficiently different from other investments so that it requires special public action.

Right after World War I, for example, there was an extreme housing shortage in many parts of this country. In order to encourage the creation of more housing, governments provided subsidies in one form or another. New York State was in the forefront of this effort, and in 1920 its legislature passed a law to alleviate the critical housing shortage by granting a ten-year real-estate tax exemption for new residential construction. Yet the ten-year exemption neither encouraged the production of the amount of housing needed nor stimulated housing production for the economic sector of the population most in need of housing. Accordingly, in 1925, New York State passed the Limited Dividends Housing Law, creating a state board of housing and providing for both public and private limited-dividend corporations. Its purposes were to promote the investment of private funds at low interest rates and the construction of new housing facilities under public supervision. The act also expanded and continued the tax-exemption policy of the 1920 Act, but only for the limited-dividend corporations whose earnings were limited to 6 percent of their investment. Maximum rents were also fixed.

As early as the 1920s, therefore, the state of New York had introduced a limit on profits, a limit on rents, and provided inducements to bring private capital into the market. Soon after, however, the country stood in the midst of a depression so serious that, regardless of the inducements, the private sector could not produce the needed housing. As a consequence, a number of states in the early and mid-1930s enacted laws that empowered cities, counties, and municipalities to set up local housing authorities with broad powers to undertake slum clearance and to build low-rent projects. Such authorities were generally exempted from state and local taxes. They were also specifically authorized to plan, construct, reconstruct, improve, alter, or repair housing projects, and to take over and operate projects by lease or purchase, exercise powers of eminent domain, and take any action necessary to obtain federal aid in the financing of such projects.

In the 1930s the federal government was also active in the housing field. Its role is best understood when the economics of housing are made clear. Housing is a highly labor-intensive capital investment. A generally accepted rule of thumb is that two-thirds of the construction cost is in labor, and one-third is in materials, though some contend that 80 percent of the cost of construction is in the cost of labor. Accordingly, in the 1930s the federal government's first efforts were directed toward stimulating employment by providing Reconstruction Finance Corporation (RFC) loans to private housing developers. The RFC later transferred these duties to the Public Works Administration, which also engaged in direct federal ownership programs. But the programs were restricted by a scarcity of funds and by a court decision denying the Public Works Administration the power to use eminent domain for slum-clearance purposes. This adverse court decision, as well as other factors, added to the widespread sentiment that public housing and slum clearance were appropriately state and local responsibilities and that the federal government should only be a money lender.

The United States Housing Act of 1937 was passed in this context and was the basic pattern of federal assistance for low-income housing that continued essentially unchanged until its recent demise. It authorized federal aid to states, municipalities, and local public-housing authorities, and left the construction, ownership, and management of the public-housing projects to the local agencies. During the next three decades the federal, state, and local governments enacted a number of programs providing subsidies, not only for low-income housing, but also for moderate and middle-income housing. Basically these programs fell into three categories: (1) direct loans and periodic subsidies by states for the construction and operation of low income housing; (2) direct loans to private limited-profit and nonprofit corporations for the construction of middle-income rental and cooperative housing; and (3) loans and subsidies or direct capital grants to urban-renewal agencies to assist in financing the local cost of federally aided urban-renewal projects.

While most of this local housing legislation was couched in language using the terms low rent and low income the legislatures in most instances never clearly defined these terms. Instead, statutes established ratios of income to rental that defined eligibility in terms of the ability of the prospective tenants to pay for such housing. This was important because the courts, in interpreting the terms "low rent" and "low income," repeatedly held that the terms did not mean the lowest possible rents or persons of the lowest income. Rather, eligibility lists could include all of those persons and families whose housing needs could not be met by the unaided operations of private enterprise. What this meant was that some middle-income people benefited from these projects, and they began to back some publicly assisted housing programs.

While the states and the courts were establishing a broad interpretation of eligibility for public housing, the United States Housing Act of 1937 defined "families of low income" to mean families in the lowest income group who could not afford to pay enough to cause private enterprise in their locality or metropolitan area to build an adequate supply of decent, safe, and sanitary dwellings for their use. Subsequent federal housing legislation and programs sought to induce the creation of housing for families whose incomes exceeded local public-housing limits. Over the years, therefore, a number of programs established income limits at various percentages of income or in some relation to public-housing limits.

A review of programs to encourage the creation of new or the renovation of old housing shows that subsidies generally correspond with four major financial problem areas.[2] The first area is the land. The cost as well as the availability of land necessarily affects the ability to produce housing and the cost of such housing production. Governmental programs that used eminent domain made land in many metropolitan areas available at an almost nominal cost. The standard in the Eastern states or in Chicago where I worked was $500 per dwelling unit, a figure so low that little more could be done about land cost to produce a significant reduction in the cost of housing.

A second area was taxes, and specifically real estate taxes. As a general rule, real-estate taxes in most central cities constitute approximately 20 percent of one's average monthly rent. Some communities, though not many, provide tax abatement or tax exemption for new or rehabilitated housing. But under present economic conditions, it seems unlikely that other cities or metropolitan areas will provide tax abatement or exemption as a method of aiding the production of housing.

The third area is the cost of construction. Construction is a highly labor-intensive capital expenditure, and when dealing with state or government programs, one must pay prevailing wage rates, which usually means union wage rates. At least two programs attempted to deal with this housing cost factor.

The first was a small demonstration project called Rapid Rehabilitation. It was undertaken to test the feasibility of providing housing in rehabilitated old tenements to low-income families in New York City through a speedy and economical rehabilitation system combining advanced engineering techniques and preassembled components. Under the program, a building was gutted and rehabilitated in seventy-two hours. At that time the total cost of recent new public-assisted housing was running between $17,000 and $21,000 per unit, while Rapid Rehabilitation development cost came to $26,400 per unit. Because of its high cost the project was terminated.

The second program in this area was developed in Pennsylvania as a housing assistance program. While the first program was devised to make construction cheaper, the second dealt with a grant in a maximum amount of 35 percent of the total project cost upon the condition that for a period of twenty-eight years the owners agreed to abide by state regulation and control of rents in these projects. The Pennsylvania program did not provide developers with any return on investment; the benefit they received was the state capital contribution. Under the Pennsylvania program approximately three thousand units of low and moderate-income housing was produced at a cost to the state of $10 million. At that time the cost of producing a housing unit was about $10,000. The state contribution, therefore, was approximately $3,000 to $3,300 per housing unit and the balance of the financing came from existing Federal Mortgage Insurance Programs.[3]

These figures are important because those units were really marvelous and served the population intended. The numbers could hardly be duplicated now. But this was also a program that worked.

Of course the fourth problem area in subsidy efforts is the cost of money or credit. Credit is a predominant factor in the construction, purchase, and transfer of housing. Changes in interest rates and in the availability of credit affect the price of housing services more than the price of most other capital consumer goods. Several years ago, for example, a ½ percent increase in interest rates meant a $4 per month increase in rent per room. In other words, if you had a four-room apartment and you had a ½ percent interest rate increase, you had to charge the tenant a $20 per month rent increase. Obviously, because construction costs have since increased materially, a similar ½ percent increase in interest rate would result in a significantly higher rental increase.

It is with this element, the cost of money, that most of the governmental programs—whether state or federal—have dealt. Examples that come to mind are, of course, the various state housing finance agencies. By the use of the state's credit or the state's moral obligation, and by issuing tax-exempt bonds, agencies sought to borrow at lower than normal rates and transfer the benefits to the development of housing under their particular programs. In addition, the Federal Mortgage Insurance Program provided mortgage security to encourage investment and loans. Finally, both the low-interest rate and the home-ownership programs provided a direct-interest subsidy to the developers of housing.

But by 1976 the federal programs had been shut down. The state housing finance agencies either could not borrow at all, or could not borrow at rates which could be used to produce marketable housing for low-, moderate-, or middle-income families. What was left at the federal level was the Section 8 program that, when it was brought into being by the Housing and Community Development Act of 1974, supposedly provided a package of tools which would help low and moderate-income families to obtain housing. But in two years under Section 8, we produced across the country a grand total of two hundred units of housing. The architects of that program contend that it was not designed to help produce housing, but merely to help low and moderate-income families gain access to available housing, and perhaps slightly to enlarge the stock. But because of that design the potential support for new housing programs did not materialize and the critical shortage of affordable low and moderate-income housing remained.

That all sounds grim enough. But we are also faced with one other problem that we never had before; the increasing cost of maintaining and operating property. For years you could assume that the level would increase slightly. Between 1967 and 1975, however, the cost of fuel alone went up 245 percent, and the general cost of maintaining and operating property went up practically 95 percent.

So you can see why I feel the way I do, and others agree. As Ada Louise Huxtable recently put it in *The New York Times:*

Rental subsidies aimed at a housing shortage begin to appear absurd, and as costs continue to rise the subsidies required over a twenty to forty year mortgage period become unreal. In New York and other cities, how and where to use limited subsidy funds to anchor slipping neighborhoods or to support stranded construction is an exercise in frustration and futility. Even if all the problems were clarified, and the climate changed tomorrow, present policy could hardly make a dent in the accelerating need and accumulating shortage that is hitting the poor the hardest and increasing hardship for the middle class. When the Great Society died, so did the objectives of 26 million new and rehabilitated homes that were to be achieved by 1978 and so did the policy. In the real sense of vision and goals, in its true national dimensions, housing is one of the most severe and tragic emergencies that this country faces. Disaster just strikes faster and more dramatically in New York.

NOTES

1. Charles Abrams, *The City Is the Frontier* (New York, 1965), p. 3.
2. These programs include the 221-D3 Below Market Interest Rate Program, the section 235 Home Ownership Program, the section 236 program, and currently the Housing Assistance Program.
3. Federal Mortgage Insurance Programs 608 or 207. Interest rates at that time were comparatively low.

RICHARD C. WADE

HOUSING: A Comparative View

Discussing the future of cities has been an indoor sport for Americans for the last century—indeed, even longer. In 1776, for example, Benjamin Franklin was poring over some maps of the West and came to the conclusion that there would be a great city where the Cuyahoga River flows into Lake Erie, which of course is where Cleveland is now situated. Not only would there be a great city there, he went even further and predicted with some understatement that it would be as pretty as Philadelphia.

Some Americans, however, have looked at the future of the metropolis and seen nothing down the road except unlimited disaster. Ignatius Donnelly, for example, writing in the 1880s, foresaw New York as a place of ten million people, and predicted a vast urban corridor that would stretch without interruption from Boston down the Eastern Coast to Washington, D.C. Having made that prediction, he decided he did not like the idea, so at the end of one of his novels they all go up in flames while the hero flies off in a dirigible and settles down to a pure rural life somewhere in Central Africa in a town improbably named Lincoln.

But generally Americans have seen cities in terms of bigger and bigger, if not necessarily bigger and better. And the frequently cited prediction of fifty million urban dwellers by the year 2000 is probably not far off the historical mark. A nation that began with only 5 percent of the population living in cities, and now has an urban population of over 80 percent, can be forgiven if it expects more of the same in the future. For the metropolis is, and will be for as long as we can see into the future, the heart of modern society.

This is true not only in the United States but elsewhere. No nation has really learned to control urban growth, not even those societies where one might expect the government to enforce its will without criticism or dissent. In the Soviet Union, for example, the government has control over jobs, over housing, over land, over education. Still, in the last twenty-five years the Soviets have not been able to control their own urban growth. As a member of an international committee on urban development, I remember vividly the committee's first meeting in 1952 or 1953, when we Westerners all said how our cities were growing helter-skelter and how unhappy we were about it, and the Russian delegate got up and said, "Oh, we don't have worries like that in the Soviet Union! We're not going to let that take place; we're going to hold Moscow down to four million people." Five years later we had another meeting. We voiced the same complaint about urban growth in the United States and elsewhere, and the Russian got up and said, "We don't have those problems! There's no uncontrolled growth in Moscow; we're keeping the population at five million." Five years later he was sure they could keep it between six and seven million.

This kind of runaway urban growth is just beginning to affect the developing world. Everywhere you look, throughout the globe, developing countries are entering the age of the giant metropolis, and we should expect rampant urban expansion to continue in the foreseeable future. And in the long run Third World cities are going to be very much like our own. For the force of urbanization is stronger than traditions, ideologies, or types of economies. For the past half-dozen years, I have been visiting countries with different kinds of social structures, different kinds of economies, different kinds of governments; from the right-wing dictatorship of Spain to the left-wing dictatorship of Rumania, to all kinds of societies in between: the Netherlands, Venezuela, Mexico, Great Britain, Yugoslavia, Germany, Australia, New Zealand—I have not yet, however, had the opportunity to visit Africa and Asia. But on examining these diverse and heterogeneous countries what is most striking is how much one city resembles another and how urban problems are very much the same from one city to the next.

Partly, this is because most of these countries have hired American planners, and so every mistake made in the United States is being repeated elsewhere. For example, Yugoslavia invited American academics to help plan the future of Sarajevo right after the war. So the American planners decided to build a big new industrial plant out on the outer edge of the city away from the beautiful new downtown area, which they also built. It is a wonderful urban environment as long as the wind does not blow—because the minute it does, it takes all the pollution from the plant and drops it right on the city. Every day the newspapers list the names of citizens killed by pollutants in the air, and there were never less than three names on any list during the time I was there.

There is the same problem with population growth in Yugoslavian cities as in Russian cities, and their authoritarian—or totalitarian—systems of government seem to be as helpless to cope with this problem as the government of Mexico. In that country, the peasants come off the countryside and squat along the hills on the outskirts of Mexico City. The typical pattern of settlement involves one person coming in and building a little hut, eight feet by ten feet; then a brother moves in with his family, then a sister, and so on. When I was there, I walked around these hills; here lived a quarter of Mexico City's population. There were so many people the city had to put in sewers and water mains, and the buses ran to the hills. I went to a meeting of planners the next day, and they pulled out the map (as you know, maps are part of the international language of planning, since everyone can understand them) and I asked one of the planners, "Why is it all green around the outskirts of the city? I was there yesterday, and there are lots of people there." And he smiled and said, "Ah, but, señor, they're not supposed to be there."

Or take the question of housing in Rumania. Rumania is the nearest thing to a police state I have ever visited; they make no bones about pushing people around wherever and whenever they want to. In Bucharest, a quarter of the country's population lives in that one city. As I was coming in from the airport we drove through an area of high-rise apartment towers—housing that looked exactly like bric-a-brac from the age of Dwight Eisenhower (what we were building in the 1950s, they were building in the 1970s). And I said to the taxi driver, "Those are very nice; what was there before?" "Oh, nothing," he replied, "just some gypsies." Well, gypsies comprise over ten percent of the population of Bucharest. So I said, "Tell me, where did they go?" "Well, they just went some other place," he responded. Sure enough, we came upon gypsies squatting in new locales farther down the road. Later I talked to a man who was a great critic—an underground critic—of housing in Bucharest. He confirmed my observation that the government did not seem to be relocating these people at all. When I asked what the People's Republic of Rumania did for the gypsies, he said: "They give them violins."

In short, urbanization is an immense force that no society, no ideology, no economy, has ever been able, really, to harness, and generally speaking, even understand. The real question is not whether cities will be bigger but how good or bad they will be. No need to adopt Edward Banfield's comfortable thesis in the "Unheavenly City," that cities are getting better, or to accept the Ford administration's pronouncement that, in William Simon's words, "the urban crisis is over" (we in New York have some trouble swallowing that). Despite our present problems, life in American cities is unquestionably more comfortable and conditions better than they were fifty or seventy-five years ago. But we would be foolish to turn our backs on the problems that still exist—the South Bronx, for example— or fail to recognize that a new and unprecedented urban problem has been building up since the end of World War II. A general urban malaise has settled across the country. And this urban crisis, in my judgment, is rooted in the persistence of the black ghetto in nearly every American city in both the North and the South. Every census shows ghetto areas growing larger; every census shows housing becoming more segregated. In short, every analysis shows conditions in the ghetto getting worse rather than better, and this was true even when the Great Society threw billions of dollars at it.

Why the persistence and the volatility of the ghetto? To answer this question we must recall the experience of European immigrants. Like every group of newcomers, they originally settled in the central cities and encountered what all first-generation residents of the central city, regardless of nationality or creed, discovered, namely wretched schools, inadequate housing, vice, crime, endemic disorder. The genius of American society allowed millions of people from different lands, people speaking different languages and having different cultures and religions, to enter American life and ultimately join the metropolitan mainstream. After establishing an economic foothold, they began to move out from the old concentrated areas and disperse throughout the metropolitan area. Within a generation or two the journey upward and outward was the realizable dream of a substantial percentage of the immigrant population.

We all know full well the experience of the Irish, the Germans, and the Italians in this city, and of immigrants in other cities where the numbers of Poles or Czechs or other groups are large. The model was the same everywhere. The downtown area, which was the staging ground for this upward and outward mobility, was never a very pleasant place to live. It was filled with all the problems I have already mentioned, plus a few others that no longer exist. But these conditions were tolerable to the immigrant because he thought of them as temporary. He knew somebody in the neighborhood who had made it out; someone in the church, or at school, an uncle, or maybe even a member of the immediate family. There is now a lot of nostalgic literature about the "good old neighborhood," usually written from a vantage point thirty years and thirty miles removed. But the universal impulse, back then, was to get out as fast as possible.

When blacks and Puerto Ricans began to move into America's northern cities, it was assumed that they would go through the same escape process the immigrants had gone through. There was therefore no public policy to help the transition because it was assumed to be automatic and inevitable. It was assumed that blacks and Hispanics would, in fact, gather in the center, which they did. But then, of course, came the big difference between the old ghetto and the new. Instead of serving as a staging area for population dispersal, the ghetto simply moved out block by block, overtaking old white neighborhoods and spreading across most of downtown. This was something new. By 1920, in Chicago, half the Italians lived outside the old Italian area; by 1950, half the Italians were living outside the city limits in the metropolitan area. But in the case of black migration to that city, the ghetto simply got bigger, oozing out into the areas immediately surrounding it.

The black experience, in short, has been significantly different from the immigrant experience. And it has had two consequences. The first is its impact on the black middle class. This is a substantial group of people. In fact, no group has produced a middle class as rapidly as have the blacks in northern cities. In 1950 the census disclosed that the black middle class comprised 7.8 percent of the black population in the cities. By 1960 that figure had risen to 17.8 percent; by 1970, to 33 percent. Although successful in the classic American sense of pulling themselves up by their own bootstraps, they have been denied the one thing that is a symbol of success in the United States: the right to live in a neighborhood of their own choosing, to settle in a community with schools and facilities equal to their and their children's ambitions. That right they have been denied, and they now know why. They have the money; they have the jobs; they have the education and skills. But their skins are black. They have become the indelible immigrants.

Since they are not able to move, the ghetto in which they are imprisoned just moves outward and grows inexorably larger. The black middle class has produced some of the most embittered people in the country. All through the fifties and sixties, it was extraordinary to see the high level of education among leaders of the civil rights movement—the Whitney Youngs, the Roy Wilkinses, the Martin Luther Kings. They were all from the middle class. Despite undeniable and substantial gains achieved under their leadership—desegregation, voter registration, affirmative-action programs, fair housing laws—there has been a slow realization throughout the entire black community, but particularly among members of the black middle class, that social mobility in the black population is largely vertical, not horizontal. Atlanta's "Mink Ghetto" is typical of a situation that obtains in every large American city in both North and South: block after block of fifty-, sixty-, and seventy-thousand-dollar homes inhabited entirely by black families who can afford to live elsewhere but are unable to. These people are naturally embittered, as you can well imagine. Some of the worst cocktail conversation I have ever heard has come from middle-class blacks on the subject of race and residential restrictions.

So the first consequence of the persistence of the ghetto has been the embitterment of successful middle-class blacks. The second consequence has been the impact of permanent containment on young blacks. Both parents and children have concluded that the ghetto is permanent, not a temporary staging ground for outward mobility. And now the children are asking, "What difference does it make if I stay in school, avoid youthful indulgences, get an education, get a job, make a good income? I would end up just like the guys down the street. They come home at night, lock the door ten times, and hope nothing happens by morning." Every one of our programs in the inner city, in my judgment, has broken down on this question of motivation. Social workers are always asking, "They don't seem motivated. Why can't they do what the Italians, the Poles, the Jews, and everyone else did." The answer is very simple: They have not been treated like Italians, Poles, Jews, and others.

I come from an Irish-Catholic family. We lived in five different residences in the Chicago metropolitan area, each one nicer than the one before, each farther out in the suburbs. My father paid little attention to the old neighborhood. He sent some money back to his church until the depression, he joined the Ancient Order of Hibernians and made a damned fool of himself every St. Patrick's Day; but aside from this, his orientation was entirely toward the suburbs and not toward the old neighborhood. Middle-class blacks, on the other hand, have not been given that luxury.

The emergence of the permanent ghetto places a heavy burden on another group: working-class whites. These are people who have moved two or three times already but lack the resources to move again. The guerilla warfare between black and white that takes place on the streets and in the schools occurs most frequently in areas where black and white neighborhoods overlap. Coming to terms with race and the ghetto is perhaps the single most urgent piece of unfinished business facing our society, and yet we ask those least able to handle the problem to be the most accommodating. Our society expects whites with the lowest incomes, the least education, the least security to do most of the day-to-day coping with the most challenging domestic issue of our time. Meanwhile, out in the suburbs, those with high education, high income, and high security can look back and debate the question of race and the ghetto with smug detachment, complaining about the militancy of blacks and dubbing the whites "blacklashers."

Let us look at the whole question of housing in this connection, because so much hangs on it. We need a long-range housing policy with a view to slowing down the outward growth of the permanent ghetto and ultimately reducing and even eliminating it. We need a practical policy, in other words, that will come to grips with this most critical of social issues with a minimum of disruption and coercion and a maximum of fairness for everyone concerned.

As the nation proceeds into the last quarter of the twentieth century, we find weak areas in our economy, and the weakest for some time now has been the housing sector. People who make it their business to look at the national economy have always placed great emphasis on housing. In 1968, for example, Senator Paul Douglas and the housing commission he headed reported that, just to stay even, our housing stock would have to replace itself at the rate of two million new units every year for a decade. Since then, the replacement figures have averaged less than half that—which means that we are falling behind every year in simply maintaining the stock we had before, without really retiring much of the substandard stock. Moreover, as the demand for low and moderate-income housing increases, so does the per-unit cost of constructing such housing. It costs $50,000 today to construct one unit of housing. At that rate, even the middle class has been priced out of the new housing market. And there is reason to believe that these costs will continue to rise.

New York City alone is losing forty thousand housing units a year. And what I am talking about in New York is also true almost anywhere else.

Chicago has an even higher percentage of abandonment than New York. Similar figures can be cited for Cleveland, St. Louis, or San Francisco. And what is true of the larger cities is also true of smaller cities like Newark, Gary, and Akron. What I am talking about is a nationwide housing crisis on a grand scale.

What can we do about it? The first thing, I think, is simply to acknowledge the problem. We tend to go to great lengths to avoid coming to grips with the correlation between racism and the ghetto. We talk one year of quality education, the next year about cleaning up the environment, and so on—but inevitably we will have to return to the problem of what to do about the ghetto. So the sooner we become aware that this is the fundamental question, the better. If we flinch from meeting it head on, American society will be in real jeopardy. Although there have been few riots or general uprisings in the ghetto during the past several years, it is important to understand that such quiescence comes from resignation and despair and not because we have achieved a new level of social justice. The ghetto in the heart of every great American city ticks away like a time bomb.

My strategy for dealing with the problem of housing and the ghetto calls for a multiple approach. My first proposal envisions the creation of a new national housing policy that would link the building of low and moderate-income housing with middle-and upper-income units. Stated simply, the policy would require any developer seeking government subsidies for multifamily dwellings to reserve 15 percent of all units for low-and moderate-income families. Whether an apartment complex be located in Manhattan or in Westchester County, in the city center or the suburbs, the requirement would apply. This policy would eventually do away with the permanent ghetto. And from the point of view of people trapped in the inner city, such a policy would, at long last, provide a truly effective means of escape. People would have a choice, regardless of income, to live in various parts of the metropolis.

More important, from the standpoint of the larger society, a policy encouraging scatter-site housing would put the burden of accommodation on all communities equally. One of the great drawbacks of our housing strategy in the last years of the 1960s was its tendency to concentrate on some communities and bypass others. Warren, Michigan, for example, was singled out for special attention by George Romney during his tenure as Secretary of Housing and Urban Development. Warren is a working-class community, and the reaction of most white residents to HUD's experiment was, "Why us—why not also Grosse Point? why should we have to shoulder the burden when a richer community is much better equipped to handle the problems of accommodation?"

There is some merit to that argument. The ghetto concentrates social pathologies in one place. Suffering from bad schools, bad housing, bad sanitation facilities, noncompetitive shopping, inadequate police and fire protection and medical care, the inner-city slum is overwhelmed by pathologies that reinforce one another. A strategy of scatter-site housing would allow low and moderate-income families to take advantage of social services normally denied them without straining these services to the breaking point. Instead of a vicious cycle of social pathologies we would have a beneficial spiral of social betterment—an antipoverty program, in effect based on sharing and diffusing the burden of accommodation throughout society.

This is a long-range strategy in that immediate implementation would only gradually do away with the ghetto. But as we all know, there are other and more immediate urban problems that should and must be dealt with soon, before matters get any worse. And far from being amenable only to long-term solutions, these other problems can be dealt with by measures whose implementation will bring immediate relief. I would like to suggest some of these measures.

First, a new national urban policy should include the federalization of health and welfare. Though historically these programs originated in a few progressive states, they are now nationally mandated from Washington and hence should be sustained by federal funds. This single change, incidentally, would wipe out New York's annual deficit. The massive northern migration of southern blacks in this century—a process that accelerated enormously after World War II—profoundly altered the social structure of the metropolis. Just as white city dwellers reached middle-class status and left the city for the good life in the suburbs, the newcomers arrived. Mostly poor and having little education or skills, they were tax consumers rather than tax producers. They needed help on a large scale—and most of all they needed jobs—but industry and commerce had followed the outward movement of people. At just the time municipal governments faced additional responsibilities, they saw their revenue base shrinking. To complicate matters, federal tax policies dating from the New Deal have been taking revenues out of northern cities and spending them in the so-called sunbelt, thus creating a situation where northern tax dollars subsidize an increasingly prosperous Dixie while having to care for and educate its discards. Federalizing health and welfare would provide a national solution to what is essentially a national problem.

Another problem that has received widespread attention of late, as New York's recent fiscal crisis has so dramatically emphasized, is the whole question of the integrity of municipal bonds and, by extension, the general soundness and viability of our municipal fiscal structures. I would recommend that the best way to ensure their integrity would be for the federal government to guarantee them. This need require only the fiscal monitoring of the cities that issue the bonds. The Securities and Exchange Commission already provides this function for the investor in the private market. If we had had such a system in the past, New York's problem would have been caught in 1969, when it was manageable, instead of 1975, when it was not.

We also need federal programs that provide incentives for city and suburban cooperation. At present, federal policy continues to underwrite competition between the two parts of the metropolis. In almost every area of the country the urban crisis has moved into the tangential suburbs. Older shopping centers lose customers to the newer ones farther out from the city. As the young move farther out into the new suburbs, the inner suburbs are left with an aging population whose income, though often substantial, can no longer support a full range of governmental services. Crime rates—that special symbol of inner-city decay—have gone up twice as rapidly in the inner suburbs as in cities. These and other examples of the spread of inner-city problems into the suburbs have not persuaded many suburban dwellers, nor the federal government, of their *metropolitan* nature, and the wisdom of encouraging policies that underwrite cooperation rather than competition.

Finally, we need to change federal tax policies that since the Roosevelt administration have been pumping money into the South. I do not mean by this that the Northeast, and New York City in particular, be the only beneficiaries of reapportioned cash flows, or that Dallas-Fort Worth, which will have their own metropolitan problems in the not-too-distant future, ought to be starved. But there must be a conscious effort to help those cities presently most in need wherever located.

PART THREE

PLANNING AND PRACTICE:
Health Care

THE EDITORS

OVERVIEW AND PREVIEW

The dismantling of the Kennedy-Johnson urban programs by the Nixon-Ford administrations did not curtail the attack on urban problems at local and state levels. Local politicians, because of their responsibility for and sensitivity to the continuing urban crisis, have been particularly active in seeking to ease the variety of difficulties confronting the metropolis. Persistent voter rejection of increased property taxes for schools, for example, has led many office holders to appeal to state governments (already caught in their own budget crunches) for special assistance to bail out hard-pressed local educational and social-service programs. Other cities have required all public employees to live within the confines of the municipal corporation boundaries in a desperate attempt to recapture tax money drained into the suburbs by the outward flow of population. Even construction of convention centers, a practice once confined to major cities, spread in the past decade to smaller places as they strove to provide jobs for unskilled and semiskilled workers trapped in the inner districts of medium-sized cities. Yet each of these solutions fell short in part because each represented an attempt to devise a specific solution for a particular problem. Each failed, in short, because policy makers failed to escape from the conceptual straitjacket out of which developed the one-problem, one-solution approach in the first place, despite the widespread recognition of the interdependence of metropolitan problems.

This is not to say that in the past decade there have not been attempts to go beyond the traditional format of fitting particular programs to particular needs. Indeed, the federal government's Model Cities experiment represented a bold effort at "innovative integration," a self-conscious recognition of the multidimensionality of urban problems and the need to attack in a coordinated way the constellation of housing, welfare, job, and transportation needs of low-income metropolitan neighborhoods. That approach "failed" in part because of changing federal priorities. But it also fell short because its strategy required previously separate and semiautonomous bureaucracies to work together in close coordination. This meant that Model Cities' officials spent a great deal of initial time and energy trying to break down old bureaucratic routines and to establish new avenues of communication and action, a process that not only delayed program development and implementation, but also aroused animosity, suspicion, and frustration among the officials to whom the experiment was entrusted.

There exists, however, one area of innovation in social programs, namely health care, in which the present does not clash so conspicuously and abrasively with the bureaucratic heritage of the past. Many experimental health-care delivery systems, like Model Cities before them, rest upon the assumption that their service populations possess multiple and interrelated needs rather than particular problems. Unlike Model Cities, however, these experiments are less encumbered by entrenched bureaucracies wedded to established routines and sworn to the defense of inherited institutional structures. In this perspective, health-service delivery systems may provide a useful model for testing the effectiveness of integrated innovation as a response to present and future public needs.

This third set of articles examines some recent organizational developments in health-service delivery. Advocates of this kind of health service no longer conceive of their task in terms of hospital care and office visits as separate units of analysis. They argue instead that the proliferation of specialties in medicine, the corresponding mushrooming of hospital services, and the expansion of referrals among medical practitioners establish health care as a constellation of specialized services that no longer separates prevention from cure, diagnosis from prescription. They also contend that the quality of health-care services cannot be considered independent of the consumer of the service. Increasingly, that is, the excellence of health care is evaluated as the outcome of an interaction between the service organization and the individual's entire social milieu. It is the specification of the various concerns of the consumer, as well as those of the supplying organization, that provides the starting point and the distinctive angle of approach for the planners of the new health-care delivery systems.

In the first of this set of articles, William L. Kissick spells out basic concerns that affect today's planning for the future health care of the nation. He identifies the three major variables inextricably linked in the effort as knowledge (the state of the medical art), financial resources, and manpower; together they present a system that must deal with and respond to consumer needs. One mechanism for this is the move toward conscientiously and systematically incorporating consumer desires and responses into health practices and plans. Kissick also draws our attention to the enlarged scope of concern that is introduced by a "health-care system plan." Previously untested programs prompt his examination of both the "proper" and most effective role the federal government, through its regulatory and funding activity, might play in such a system. Kissick notes that the federal government has the potential for being either a facilitator or an inhibitor of adequate health care for the nation. How this will be resolved is not a factor of chance, however. Federal regulations are not formed independent of outside influences. Consequently, factors establishing a balance in the interdependence of health-care practitioners, financiers, consumers, and regulators must be defined in planning for health-care delivery and what can be provided to the citizenry in terms of quality and convenience.

Kissick's essay sets the stage for the second of our articles, Malcolm Peterson's analysis of some of the difficulties in developing a rational strategy of health care planning. He pays special attention to the experience of Johns Hopkins University with health-care programs in the new town of Columbia, Maryland, and in East Baltimore. Peterson not only underscores the delicate lifeline of support that will determine the success or failure of a program, but also emphasizes the way in which cost, bureaucratic and corporate regulations, physical plant, human resources, and the social and community environment all influence the final form of a delivery system. Furthermore, Peterson stresses that the bulk of the medical services needed are routine rather than rare. Given the need for routine health care, Peterson notes that we do not have an available pool of health-care professionals—particularly doctors—who deal with routine problems.

The existence of an unmet need for general medical practitioners is not particularly surprising to the medical world. But the magnitude of the anticipated need is. In the third of our set of articles, Graze Ziem traces the development of medical specialties and the forces resulting in the shortage of general practitioners who would normally deal with the routine medical needs of the general population. Particularly important in this respect is the homogeneity of the group of people who become medical doctors. They are white, male, urban, and middle class or better in social background. Moreover, these doctors have been encouraged to specialize as a means of gaining status in the medical community. This emphasis, however, came at the expense of reducing the availability to the general public of routine health-care services. Ziem's view of the history and issues surrounding the emergence of specialists challenges the administrators of medical schools and hospitals to accept responsibility for the current shortage of needed health-care professionals and to augment their programs to deal with the anticipated shortage of the future.

Overall, this last set of articles presents the rudiments of a model for dealing with ongoing, large-scale, multifaceted problems requiring the indegration of a number of solutions, each with particular ramifications but each also in some way dependent on the other. Essential to this model is a process that not only measures the "marketability" of a solution but also relies on consumers to define how that solution may better meet their needs. It forces us to recognize the scope of the problems and the unexplored mechanisms with which current planners and practitioners will have to work, as well as the regulations which impinge upon or enhance the effectiveness of the proposed solution. At the same time, this model suggests that few groups are detached from the community of responsibility that must now grapple with the future of our society and of the metropolis in particular. For health-care services, answers will not come from medical-school administrators, insurance agencies or the federal government alone; each is part of a larger unity with the decisions of one affecting those of another. In the end, it is the recognition of this interdependence and the need to actively seek solutions based upon it that will require a "leap of faith" on the part of planners and practitioners. But it may ultimately provide the catalyst and crucible for innovation to deal with the pressing problems that currently threaten a viable future for the metropolis.

WILLIAM L. KISSICK

HEALTH POLICY:
A Challenge for Our Time

Total health expenditures in the United States during 1976 exceeded $134 billion, representing 8.6 percent of the gross national product (GNP).[1] By contrast the British National Health Service spent only 5.3 percent of their gross national product on health care. In 1970, the Social Security Administration traced the rise in national health expenditures since 1950 and made high and low projections for 1975 and 1980 (Figure 1).[2] By April 1976, we had passed the high projection of $120.1 billion, and a continuation of this trend would result in total expenditures in excess of $200 billion by 1980 (almost 11.5 percent of GNP). Worse still, some officials in HEW envisage expenditures totaling 15 percent of the gross national product (1 of every 7 dollars worth of goods and services produced in the entire economy) in the mid-1980s.

In my opinion we are perilously close to our upper limits in expenditures for health care. The name of the game must become allocation of resources, a perspective that implies *more* for some at the expense of less for others. A stark look at that kind of future has been provided by Victor R. Fuchs in his book *Who Shall Live?*[3] Nonetheless, even in a society as wealthy as our own, resources are by definition limited. Choices must be made. As a prelude to that, an assessment of where we have been is useful.

Although planning and resource allocation have evolved in a health-policy context constructed of sequential building blocks of national health policy stretching from state grants-in-aid to the National Health Planning and Resources Development Act of 1974, I shall focus on the health policy of the federal government. In examining its evolution, one finds that it developed from the 1930s to the present in five phases (Figure 2) characterized by increasing health-care expenditures as a portion of the gross national product.

FIGURE 1

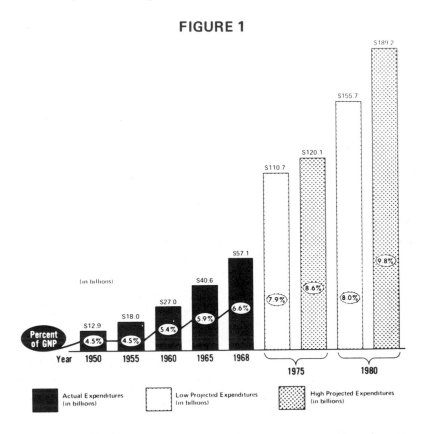

The initial thrust of national health policy focused on specialized problems such as communicable-disease control. Human misery in the depression, however, dramatized the fact that the efforts of voluntary organizations and of state and local governments were not sufficient to meet health needs, and the federal government was forced to become concerned for the health of its citizens, which it did in the Social Security Act of 1935. That legislation contained two provisions addressed to some of the widespread health needs at that time. Title V authorized grants to individual states for maternal-health and child-health programs, and

Title VI authorized annual appropriations ". . . for the purpose of assisting States in establishing and maintaining adequate public health services." Although the responsibility for seeking and obtaining health care remained the individual's, the act recognized that public assistance was required in certain cases.

FIGURE 2

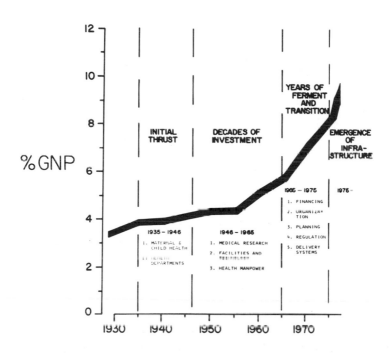

After World War II, the need for major investments in the development of basic health resources became evident. First, Congress passed the Hill-Burton Program to help communities build hospitals, public-health centers, extended-care facilities, diagnostic and treatment centers, and rehabilitation facilities. Second, Congress undertook a sustained investment in medical research through the National Cancer Institute (NCI), which though funded in 1938, began its rapid growth in appropriations in the 1950s, and through the creation of a series of other national institutes charged with conducting research on certain categories of diseases and health problems. The third health resource—manpower—attracted federal aid later than the others. It was not until 1963 that federal legislation providing support for the education of the health professions was finally passed, and subsequent mandates have followed.

For almost two decades, then, the assumption prevailed that if only sufficient funds were invested in the creation of basic health resources, the necessary services would be forthcoming. By the mid-1960s, however, it became increasingly evident to Congress that investments in resource development alone, no matter how massive, would not solve health problems. Though it registered the highest per capita expenditures for health and medical care in the world, the United States had neither the finest services nor the highest health status. That realization in the mid-1960s brought an end to complacency and a demand for solutions to existing health-care problems.

During the mid-1960s, planning, financing mechanisms, patterns of organization, and delivery systems were added to the existing responsibilities of the federal government. The Social Security Amendments of 1965, for example, initiated the effort in the United States to eliminate economic barriers to medical care. Payment by these programs of "usual and customary fees" to physicians and reimbursement of costs for hospital care followed prevailing financing mechanisms, and it was assumed that the existing health-care system could respond to the population's needs and demands if payment for services was provided.

The issues of planning and organization were addressed by means of a dozen major pieces of legislation. Community Mental Health Centers, Comprehensive Health Services for Children and Youth, the Office of Economic Opportunity, Neighborhood Health Centers, Regional Medical Programs, Comprehensive Health Planning, Professional Standards Review Organizations (PSROs), National Health Service Corps (NHSC), Health Maintenance Organizations (HMOs), Emergency Medical Systems (EMSs), Area Health Education Centers (AHECs) and the National Center for Health Services Research are all concerned primarily with a search for effective and responsive institutional mechanisms for provision of human services. In short, experiments in effective utilization of health-care resources characterized the period between 1965 and 1975, and a host of programs were authorized by Congress. Yet these parts when taken together do not form a whole. Nor, in my opinion, will financing at the federal level through National Health Insurance as now conceived provide a satisfactory health-care enterprise for our society.

Much of the discussion of National Health Insurance focuses on financing the costs of health care but fails to give adequate attention to the patterns of organizing services. There is real danger that in a desperate effort to check rising health-care costs and to curb the excesses of existing financing mechanisms, we will adopt measures that are restrictive, short-sighted, and punitive, instead of positive solutions to complex issues. The following conclusion by analysts of the national economy is equally pertinent to the health enterprise:

Without suitable incentive and reasonable allocation of its resources, a nation can fall short of getting maximum output from its manpower, capital, and "laboratory knowledge."[4]

The creation of effective programs will require an assessment of health problems in population terms to formulate and evaluate service strategies. Moreover, the performances of delivery systems will be increasingly judged by their effectiveness in improving the health of the population. It is important to remember that the demands for health services can be virtually insatiable, depending on society's level of expectation and the resources that it wishes to allocate to them. Accordingly, comprehensive health-care systems in the 1980s must accord a high priority to realizing the maximum health services from available resources and to influencing the consumers' health practices and utilization of services.

Beginning in 1975, we started to create a new infrastructure of national health services. By that time the National Health Planning and Resources Development Act of 1974 (Public Law 93-54) was in its initial phases of nationwide implementation. It begins with the assertion by Congress that "The achievement of equal access to quality health care at reasonable costs is a priority of the Federal Government," and contends that ". . . it is the purpose of this Act to facilitate the development of recommendations for a national health planning policy, to augment areawide and State planning for health services, manpower, and facilities. . . ." Congress also specifies national health priorities in the formulation of national health planning goals as follows:

Sec. 1502. The Congress finds that the following deserve priority consideration in the formulation of national health planning goals and in the development and operation of Federal, State, and area health planning and resources development programs:

(1) The provision of primary care services for medically underserved populations, especially those which are located in rural or economically depressed areas.

(2) The development of multi-institutional systems for coordination or consolidation of institutional health services (including obstetric, pediatric, emergency medical, intensive and coronary care, and radiation therapy services).

(3) The development of medical group practices (especially those whose services are appropriately coordinated or integrated with institutional health services), health maintenance organizations, and other organized systems for the provision of health care.

(4) The training and increased utilization of physician assistants, especially nurse clinicians.

(5) The development of multi-institutional arrangements for the sharing of support services necessary to all health service institutions.

(6) The promotion of activities to achieve needed improvements in the quality of health services, including needs identified by the review activities of Professional Standards Review Organizations under part B of title XI of the Social Security Act.

(7) The development by health service institutions of the capacity to provide various levels of care (including intensive care, acute general care, and extended care) on a geographically integrated basis.

(8) The promotion of activities for the prevention of disease, including studies of nutritional and environmental factors affecting health and the provision of preventive health care services.

(9) The adoption of uniform cost accounting, simplified reimbursement, and utilization reporting systems and improved management procedures for health service institutions.

(10) The development of effective methods of educating the general public concerning proper personal (including preventive) health care and methods for effective use of available health services.

In response to these priorities, work began on establishing approximately two hundred Health Systems Agencies (HSAs), each serving a Health Service Area with a population of 400,000 to 3,000,000. These nonprofit or public-benefit corporations will be responsible for developing Health Service Plans (HSPs) and Annual Implementation Plans (AIPs) for review and approval by State Health Planning and Development Agencies (SHPAs) and State Health Coordinating Councils (SHCCs). These latter agencies will develop State Health Plans (SHPs) and State Medical Facilities Plans (SMFPs) for submission to HEW. Space does not permit a review of the detailed requirements for organizing these respective agencies or their detailed functions. Undoubtedly, such complex legislation shall not want for difficulty in implementation. It is, however, fair to suggest that this synthesis of the Hill-Burton Program, the Regional Medical Programs, and Comprehensive Health Planning has set in motion the creation of a societal infrastructure for ". . . coordination of medical services."

With the enactment of the National Health Planning and Resources Development Act of 1974, the evolution of health policy entered its fourth phase. During the last three phases health-care expenditures rose from 5.2 percent of the gross national product in 1960 to 7.2 percent of

GNP in 1970 to 8.6 percent in 1976. But since health-care advocates must compete with others for a share of the gross national product, it appears that continued growth of health-care expenditures to from 12 to 15 percent of GNP will be thwarted by an unwillingness of other sectors of the economy collectively to contract their share of GNP to the vicinity of 85 percent. Whether the Health Act of 1974, which calls for a "national approach to the . . . increasing cost of health care" is successful in controlling health-care costs, it is highly probable the expenditures for housing, food, education, recreation, energy, transportation, consumer items, aerospace, and defense will combine to stem the rising tide of health expenditures in the near futre.

FIGURE 3

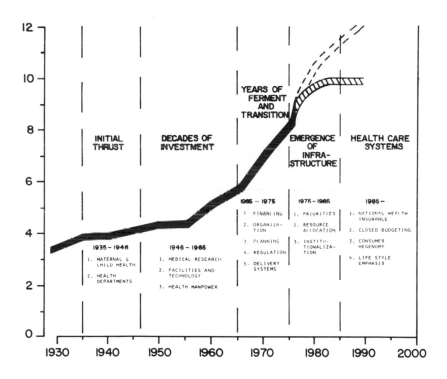

Looking back from the year 2000, one might find a scenario that sees the period of infrastructure creation (1975-1985) merging into a period of the creation of health-care systems after 1985 (Figure 3) and a gradual leveling of the cost-inflation curve. The foremost potential of the National

Health Planning and Resources Development Act of 1974 (Public Law 93-64) would appear to be found in the pursuit of the ". . . institutional infrastructure of modern organized society . . ." conceptualized by Gunnar Myrdal.[5] It can be anticipated that three major events will characterize the period of the emergence of the infrastructure:

1. *Priorities:* Goals, objectives, and priorities for health-care systems, must be formulated as a basis for options and program alternatives.

2. *Resource Allocation:* Investment choices must be made. Funds allocated to one program are not available to another. Resources by definition are limited. Choices must be made.

3. *Institutionalization:* The health-care enterprise is predominantly a small entrepreneurial industry. Approximately 80 percent of the economic units employ seven workers or less. At the other extreme the Kaiser Foundation Health Plan contracts to provide services to 3.7 million subscribers and earned $750,000,000 in 1975. Having abandoned the free-market economy, we are faced with the overwhelming task of regulating small units or providing incentives for institutionalization.

Probably most importantly, political feasibility would appear to suggest 1982-1984 as an appropriate date for enactment of National Health Insurance. Given such other high priority issues as energy, the economy, and tax reform, it is doubtful that the Ninety-fifth or Ninety-sixth Congress will be able to devote the time and energy necessary to deal with the vested interests and circumstances. The requisite negotiations and compromise on these questions will be extraordinary, and therefore the coming of the mid-80s (Would you believe 1984?) ought to usher in an era of new health-care systems made up of the following components:

1. *National Health Insurance:* only a political wizard could now predict its form. It could well be that the impact of energy policies on the auto industry could be the predominant circumstance in shaping national health insurance through labor-management bargaining of fringe benefits.

2. *Closed Budgeting:* At present extra funds flow from multiple sources. Ceilings will be imposed both in the market (energy versus health care) and through regulation (state rate setting and federal control of hospital costs).

3. *Consumer Hegemony:* Health is too important to be left to health professionals. Consumer requirements in public law will impose a corporate

form of accountability within federal and state regulation to replace the lack of accountability of the marketplace or the ballot box.

4. *Life Style:* The health-care concept of the Canadian Report (Lalonde)[6] appears likely in the future. Priority for life style, environment, and human biology over health-care organizations probably will entail budget ceilings for the last category and investment of portions of its "growth share" to life style and related programs wherein the investment could make an even greater contribution to the health of the population. The British National Health Service spends 5.6 percent of gross national product in contrast to the 8.6 percent in the United States. It is not unlikely that the superior British health experience is more related to the alternative investments in social programs of the additional 3 percent saved than to any more effective health services.

Regardless of the level of expenditures or percent of the gross national product we spend in the year 2000, we will remain on an evolutionary curve that manifests the ineraction of scientific, technical, political, managerial, institutional, and personal values and convictions.

As for the twenty first century and beyond, two glimpses can be found in Delphi Studies by the Research and Development Staff of the Smith Kline and French Corporation[7] and by McLaughlin and Sheldon in their book *The Future and Medical Care.*[8] Selected findings from these two studies are presented and those in italics merit special emphasis:

Delphi Studies,

1981-1990 - *Discovery of biochemical basis of schizophrenia.*
- Development of a cure for arthritis.
- Development of effective and safe immuno-suppressive drugs.
- Successful organ transplantation including heterologous tissues.
1991-2000 - Effective prevention of heart attacks.
- General and substantial increase in life expectancy, postponement of ageing and limited rejuvenation.
- Discovery of drugs which prevent cancer.
- Discovery of chemicals which restore elasticity in fibres in lungs and vascular muscle.
2001-2017 - *Elimination of undesirable characteristics through gene manipulation.*

      - Drugs which are capable of influencing genetic expression.
      - Major reduction in congenital defects.

McLaughlin and Sheldon

1990-1994 - A crude but effective means of genetic control.

      - Patients in special risk groups—weak hearts, diabetes, etc.— carry computer monitored radio-transmitting devices to warn of body function.

1987   - *A computer-based medical record bank covers 80% of the United States population and gives ready, accurate access to full medical records.*

1990+   - Life support and waste elimination systems are built into new houses and apartment houses.

1990-1994 - Drugs are now available to ameliorate or eliminate many forms of mental illness and some learning handicaps.

1975-1979 - Resocialization of the medical student has occurred so that his perspective includes the social variables in health and illness.

1990-1994 - Medical-social decisions are now based on accepted "qualitative" or "Happiness" measures of the quality of life rather than on morbidity or mortality.

1984   - Physicians now must undergo compulsory reexamination and relicensing.

1981   - *Solo practice has virtually disappeared except for doctors over fifty.*

1980-1994 - There is de facto federal control over psychiatric and medical facilities.

1980-1989 - Well-equipped and well-staffed health centers are strategically located to serve urban, suburban, and rural needs.

1980-1994 - We will have effective coordination of medical care disbursement and planning on a regional basis throughout the country.

1980-1989 - Medicare-type payment programs now cover better than 95% of the American population.

1994   - *Medical industry activities now account for more than 20% of GNP.*

1985   - We now have direct public participation in decision-making with "real-time" polling.

1980-1989 - *We now have broad community participation in the management of virtually all medical institutions.*

While you are reflecting on the implications of these possible future realities, let me suggest that technological advances in medicine beget as well as solve problems. Chronic renal dialysis, for example, is acknowledged to be a lifesaving benefit. However, the question of equity and social justice confront us. Present data indicate that approximately 50,000 patients (0.2) percent of the population) with end-stage kidney disease will require 1 percent of total health expenditures. What of the other 99.98 percent of the population. As Victor Fuchs asks, *Who Shall Live?* While this is a painful question to ask, it is one we answer inadvertently all the time.

Technological advance also bears other consequences. Amitai Etzioni, a noted sociologist at Columbia University, became fascinated with the discussion of genetic engineering at a meeting sponsored by the World Health Organization. His observations and concerns are presented with compelling clarity in *Genetic Fix*,[9] in which he pondered the implications of the techniques for gene selection and sex predetermination. After reviewing survey research data on sex preference, he posited that existing attitudes would result in more than 60 percent of the firstborn being male. One might ask, How many families would pair up the boy with a girl?

I'd like to close with a selection taken from *The Future and Medical Care.*[10]

New York Times Editorial: "The Threat of Science," January 30, 2000. While researchers in the health care system deserve great admiration for their discoveries in the last thirty years, and even greater admiration for their overcoming of arbitrary disciplinary divisions, they now present perhaps the greatest threat of any group to the freedom of the American people. Imbued with the sense of their own importance, they have left the field of science for the field of politics. And they have been remarkably successful. They are now second in influence only to public relations personnel.

In all fairness, it must be said that public and official support for basic research has for all purposes disappeared, leaving researchers no adequate funding for this purpose, so they have turned to politics in an effort to bring about the application of earlier advances. Their holistic approach has yielded potential solutions to many social problems. However, past implementation of their proposals has already led to serious dangers, and their plans for the future, as recently announced by the Secretary of Social Research, show real cause for alarm. Despite widespread concern on the part of the public, little has been done to protect the privacy of citizens, most aspects of whose lives are recorded in National Data Bank. Control and chemical and biological warfare weapons is largely ineffectual, and accidents are increasing.

But these are minor concerns in the light of more recent proposals. The Secretary's announced plans include the following: Introduction of genetic copying and manipulation on a mass scale to produce only "desirable" traits; birth control chemicals in the water supply, with the ultimate aim of completely vegetative human propagation; the use of chemicals for the control of personality and emotional deviations.

One wonders if the potential benefits are worth the loss of freedom involved. It is time that researchers in the various areas of health care be placed under the supervision of Congress. Their plans are too far-reaching to be considered only in the light of their potential benefits to the health of the population. Their power must be limited.

For me, the year 2000 will—if present policies hold—signal mandatory retirement from the faculty of the University of Pennsylvania. Speculating on the validity of the *New York Times* editorial of January 30, 2000, I look back twenty-three years to my medical-student days and recall the words of a biochemistry professor. "Fifty percent of what we teach you will be wrong. Unfortunately, we don't know which fifty percent." And so, on the the twenty-first century. En route, I would caution, watch out for 1984!

NOTES

1. National Center for Health Statistics, *Health United States 1975* (Rockville, Maryland, 1975).
2. Social Security Administration, *Research and Statistics Note* (Washington, D.C., 1970).
3. Victor R. Fuchs, *Who Shall Live?* (New York, 1974).
4. W. Hitch and R. N. McKean, *The Economics of Defense in a Nuclear Age* (New York, 1965).
5. Gunnar Myrdal, *Beyond the Welfare State* (New Haven, 1960).
6. Marc Lalonde, *A New Perspective on the Health of Canadians* (Ottawa, Canada, 1974).
7. A. D. Bender, A. E. Strack, G. W. Ebright, and G. von Haunalter, "Delphi Study Examines Developments in Medicine," *Futures* (June 1969).
8. Curtis P. McLaughlin and Alan Sheldon, *The Future and Medical Care* (Cambridge, Mass., 1974).
9. Amitai Etzioni, *Genetic Fix* (New York, 1973).
10. McLaughlin and Sheldon, p. 89.

MALCOLM L. PETERSON

HEALTH CARE: The Columbia
and East Baltimore,
Maryland, Experience

Expenditures for health care, soon to exceed $150 billion per year, account for over 8 percent of the gross national product. For the past decade, the share of payments for health care by local or national governmental agencies has risen rapidly, and defending against the encroachment of these fiscal demands on the other budgetary priorities of government is now commonplace in city councils, state legislatures, and congressional committees. Any consideration of "the future of the metropolis" must address the circumstances of our system of health care for the inhabitants of the metropolis. But it is also necessary to look under that system to be sure that what is happening in the provision of health services is what is needed. In other words, are we getting what we think we are paying for? Not only do I believe that we are not, but even if we were, we are paying far too much for it.

To explicate the basis of that statement, one should first consider the general needs for personal health care and then examine the ways in which our personnel, institutions, and money are mobilized to meet those needs. Our knowledge of the true needs for health care is meager. Generally, we measure needs in terms of utilization of services; in the United States, this measure is especially inadequate because we do not precisely know the determinants of use of services. In Figure 1 is shown a representation of the general pattern of utilization of services. Out of each 1,000 persons in our country, about 720 have contact with the health-care system in a year. About 100 enter a hospital at least once, and 10 of these enter a hospital in a major academic medical center. This last figure is a commentary

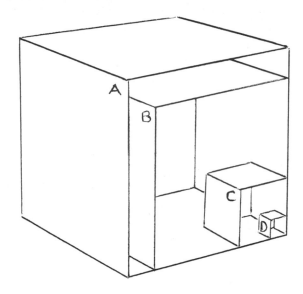

Figure 1: Utilization of health services. This volumetric representation of the use of the medical care system in the United States illustrates the relative frequency of contact of 1,000 persons (Cube A) with that system during a year: 720 persons (Cube B) actually have at least one contact with the system, 100 persons (Cube C) are admitted to a hospital at least once in the year, and 10 individuals (Cube D) are admitted to teaching hospitals. See L. K. White, "Life and Death and Medicine," *Scientific American*, 229 (1973), pp. 23-33.

TABLE 1

Profile of family practice in Virginia

Conditions for Which Patient Is Seen	Percentage of All Visits
upper respiratory infections	10.3
check-up	8.4
hypertension	5.7
lacerations, contusions, and abrasions	4.0
depressive neurosis, anxiety neurosis, psychophysiologic disorders	3.5
sprains and strains	2.4
diabetes mellitus	2.4
obesity	2.0

Based on 526,196 visits to 118 family physicians. See note 1 for complete profile of these family practices.

on the "reality" of the teaching environment from which emanates the next generation of physicians and other providers of health services to the population-at-large. Concentration on "interesting cases" prepares physicians, especially those who are studying to be specialists and sub-specialists, to provide excellent responses to complex technical demands posed by certain pathological conditions. Are such responses what is needed for those other 990 persons? Probably not for most, judging by what are the most frequent problems among the roughly two-thirds of the population whose contact with the medical-care system entails being seen in the office of a general practitioner (Table 1). After subtracting from the 567 separate problems seen in general practice, those that are most common, there remain 545 (Figure 2). In other words, health needs that consume large portions of physicians' work-hours are uncommon in the teaching environment, are often most related to behavioral or social circumstances, and are mostly not immediately life-threatening but involve self-limited or incurable diseases.

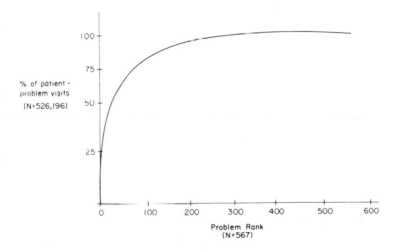

Figure 2: Cumulative frequency of patients' problems as reflected in aggregate family practice. Note that 50% of the patient visits to family practitioners in the State of Virginia are related to the 22 most frequent of the 567 different problems which were the basis of the office visits.

Because the United States health system is chiefly a "cottage industry," it is, therefore, difficult to know, for a defined populace of a single metropolis, what the health needs are. We are stuck with a very poor starting point in the development of a rational strategy of health care. Circumstances for planning are a little better in the United Kingdom because the general practitioner is the focal point of care for a group of persons who enroll as the identified population receiving care. The size of that population in the average general practice is about twenty-five hundred persons. In any given year, among that average group of persons, there will occur a number of health and disease problems which have been enumerated (Table 2). Probably these are characteristic of people in United States metropolitan areas; on the basis of such knowledge, we could design a system of health care that would be effective, economical, and would satisfy both clients and providers of care. The staffing of the system, design and location of institutions, and fiscal elements could be arranged on the basis of need and appropriate response. Such a strategy has been the foundation of recent legislation creating agencies that are supposed to be responsible for planning health care in the various regions of the nation. But caution is necessary in developing plans for health care of different populations. The average population derived from a profile of a homogeneous microcosm does not exist in the actual macrocosm. Residents of mobile, middle-class communities have very different health needs than those of a predominantly working-class or impoverished community. Mental illness, high blood pressure, eye problems, heart disease, and conditions causing mental retardation are more common among people in the lower socioeconomic strata. Older people have greater numbers of health problems, and their use of health services is qualitatively as well as quantitatively different from younger persons for whom preventive care, such as immunizations and family planning, and normal status, such as pregnancy and childhood, pose different requirements.

Several years ago, The Johns Hopkins University became involved in opportunities to develop programs of health care for two quite different communities. In the new planned city of Columbia, Maryland, its health system was designed at the same time as the city itself became populated. This system was conceived along the lines of a prepaid group practice, similar to the Kaiser plans that evolved in the western United States at the start of World War II. The principle of a group of salaried physicians providing a comprehensive range of health services to a defined set of families in return for a uniform annual sum of money appears to be an American contribution to health systems. In Columbia, this design evolved from a partnership between an insurance company, medical school, and a teaching hospital.[3] The benefits provided in return for the annual premium included most services, except dental care and cosmetic surgery, and did not cover unlimited hospital use. In an affluent community of new residents with many children and few elderly persons, the patterns of health problems are not unexpected (Table 3); the frequency of these problems is not unlike the observations in general practice.[4] Physicians are not necessarily the best category of personnel to provide many of the services attendant upon such needs as well baby care, management of obesity or alcoholism, or treatment of fairly stable chronic diseases. Nonphysicians (health associatesand nurse practitioners) have been employed and are successfully delivering a major portion of care.[5]

TABLE 2
Profile of a General Practice in Great Britain

Condition for Which Patient Is Seen	Persons seen per year in a Typical General Practice of 2,500 Enrolled Patients
upper respiratory infection	500
gastrointestinal problems	250
skin disorders	225
acute tonsillitis	100
rheumatic and arthritic conditions	100
otitis media	75
wax impacted in ear canal	50
urinary tract infections	50
acute bronchitis and pneumonia	50
hypertension	25
coronary artery disease	20
diabetes	10
acute myocardial infarctions	7
all new cancers	5
lung cancer	1-2
breast cancer	1
cervical cancer	1 every 3 years
lymphoma	1 every 15 years

Only selected conditions are identified. See note 2 for the complete profile.

All of these nonphysicians are effective and accepted in the other community health system, the East Baltimore Medical Plan, in which Johns Hopkins is a partner, but that was not always so. When the physicians at

Johns Hopkins suggested to the Board of Directors of this prepaid group practice organized for inner-city residents that midwives would provide good obstetrical services, the negative rejoinder was backed up by the question, "How many midwives are working in Columbia?" Since the effort to hire a midwife there had thus far been futile, the answer "none" sufficed to end the discussion. When growth of the membership calls for additional obstetrical staff, this suggestion would probably have a different fate now that midwives *are* working in Columbia and health associates have proven themselves to be effective primary-care practitioners in both programs.

TABLE 3

Profile of Internal Medicine Practice in an HMO

Condition for Which Patient Is Seen	Percentage of All Visits
upper respiratory infection	10.9
sore throat	5.5
nasal problems	4.8
hypertension	4.4
dermatitis	3.8
abdominal pain	3.4
chest pain	2.7
depression	2.4
back pain	2.0
heart disease	2.0
headaches	2.0
pneumonia	2.0
lacerations	2.0
diabetes	1.7
gastroenteritis	1.7
urinary tract infection	1.7
normal examination	1.7
	54.9

Based on 293 visits to adult medicine. See note 6 for the more complete profile of the comprehensive practice.

Two of the greatest lessons from the two health plans relate to the issues of finances and control. In Columbia, the subscribers pay for their services through direct payment of premiums from their own pockets or, more commonly, through their employers as standard health benefits plus payroll deduction. The administration of such financial arrangements is familiar and fairly standard. However, in East Baltimore, the range of fiscal means for the enrollees is limited and often provided from highly restricted third-party payments. Since Medicaid does not pay for most services for persons seeking preventive care, and Medicare does not pay for drugs, the only way impoverished persons eligible for just these governmental insurance programs have their other health services paid for is by a grant to the health plan.[7] Even with the grant, there has been no means by which all residents in this neighborhood can receive health care from the East Baltimore Medical Plan, simply because the grant is not large enough to pay for all "uncovered" services for all residents without other medical insurance. This complex system of funding results in a cumbersome and expensive administrative mechanism to enable to assure that only appropriate and authorized use of funds has transpired.

Although related, the issue of control is not inseparable from finances. In its evolution in the hands of its board of directors, the East Baltimore Medical Plan has not evidently affected the quality of health care. Although the slow rate of growth of the plan, since it opened in 1971, and many of the difficulties encountered along the way can be attributed to lay directorship, the fiscal and management problems have not been overcome any more readily in other prepaid group practices organized to serve mostly low-income, inner-city residents.

Evidence is now available that leads one to hope it is realistic (1) to strive for the creation of a system of health care that offers a uniform range of health-care services to all, regardless of their social and economic circumstances, (2) to expect that the system can be operated by personnel who are humane as well as technically competent, and (3) to strive for economic controls that can increase effectiveness and reduce costs of care. Repeated observations[8] have confirmed that persons receiving care in prepaid group practices have less expenditures for their total health care than do those who receive care in the conventional fee-for-service circumstances of noncoordinated care. In part, this is a consequence of less surgery, fewer hospital admissions, and greater use of office care. Although employed persons have been those for whom the prepaid group practice design has been chiefly intended, Medicaid recipients enrolled in such prepaid group practices have received their care at less cost than comparable persons receiving care from the usual fee-for-service system.[9]

Nurse practitioners, health associates, and other "new health professionals" provide high quality care at low cost and in a fashion that is responsive to the psychological and social, as well as physiological, needs of the patients.[10] Whether or not these new health professionals will become a cornerstone in the health-care system remains to be seen. Aside from the impediments of professional nonacceptance and restrictions on their reimbursement by third-party medical insurance, the new health professionals may be displaced from the manpower pool by an oversupply

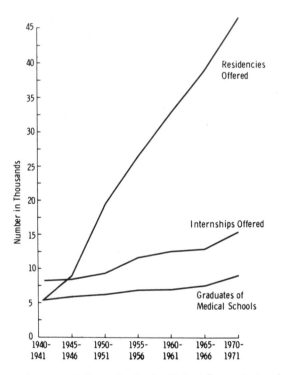

Figure 3: Postgraduate medical training in the United States during the last three decades. Before 1945, most physicians did not take specialty training in addition to their required internship.

of physicians, even though their functions are not interchangeable. The emphasis on preparation of more primary-care physicians, especially in family practice, has been forecast to bring an end to the simultaneous trend toward provision of primary care with teams of physicians and nonphysicians.

The birth of specialism in residency training programs after World War II (Figure 3) resulted in a rapid decrease in the supply of general practitioners (Figure 4). If the revitalization which is being attempted in family practice can reverse this shift toward specialism, especially in surgical and subspecialty areas, professional territoriality may offset cost containment in the design of the strategy of the health-care system. Although this struggle for control of the medical-care system between society and the profession has its roots far back in history, the recent battle in the United States has produced some vivid portents of the future as we strive for better health care. In their rejection of "a right to health care" many members of the medical profession insisted that health care is a privilege. The AMA's resistance to national health insurance goes back

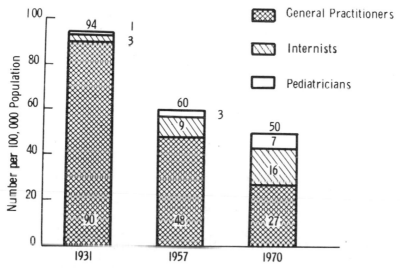

Figure 4: Availability of primary care physicians. Despite the growth in the number of physicians, there has been a steady decline in the number of general practitioners. Even in the past decade, this trend has not been reversed, although more internists and pediatricians are now being prepared so that the number of all primary care practitioners has increased slightly over that shown for 1970.

fifty years, and in the current debates, the legacy of the dual standard of care between "charity" and "private" patients is still evident. Unbridled escalation of medical-care costs and concerns about the quality of care have stimulated efforts to contain costs by getting second opinions for surgery, by forming professional standard review organizations (PSRO), by writing generic-drug-prescribing laws, and by establishing rate-setting agencies. It is clear from the experience with Medicare and Medicaid that a national health-insurance program that simply assures payment for services in the present mode is not sufficient to achieve the goals of a single standard of health care for all at reasonable cost, effectiveness, and quality. The plethora of legislative proposals on national health insurance reflect the general perception that we must find a solution to our health-care problems and that it is not yet forthcoming by an insurance mechanism which does not also effect some constraints. Since it is society that is paying these bills, and since they are becoming intolerable in the present circumstance, I predict a satisfactory outcome for the metropolis, namely, that the control will be in the hands of the residents of the metropolis and the health services will be provided with better relationship between the needs and the responses.

Simply wresting control is not enough, however. The wisdom of those in control depends on their understanding of all options in order to make the best choices. This means that the residents of a community must demand from the professionals that they be informed. We do not now have data pertinent to some of the questions that are basic to establishing public policy, but what is known certainly dictates the need for a change in some of our policies.

NOTES

1. D. Marsland, M. Wood, and F. Mayo, "A Data Bank for Patient Care, Curriculum, Research in Family Practice: 526,196 Patient Problems," *Journal of Family Practice*, 3 (1976), pp. 25-28.

2. J. Fry, *Present State and Future Needs of General Practice* (London, 1973).

3. R. M. Heyssel and H. M. Seidel, "The Johns Hopkins Experience in Columbia, Maryland," *New England Journal of Medicine*, 295 (1976), pp. 1225-1231.

4. Marsland and Wood, "A Data Bank . . . ."

5. M. L. Peterson, "Interdependence: How Can the Team Play the Game?" in V. W. Lippard and E. F. Purcell, eds., *Intermediate-Level Health Practitioners* (New York, 1973), pp. 30-45.

6. D. Steinwachs, S. Shapiro, R. Yaffe, D. Levine, and H. Seidel, "The Role of the New Health Practitioners in a Prepaid Group Practice: Change in the Distribution of Ambulatory Care between Physician and Non-physician Providers of Care," *Medical Care*, 14 (1976), pp. 95-120.

7. R. J. Blendon, "The Age of Discontinuity: The Financing of Innovative Health Care Problems in Poverty Areas," *Johns Hopkins Medical Journal*, 128 (1971), pp. 24-29.

8. M. Roemer and W. Shovich, "HMO Performance: The Recent Evidence," *Milbank Memorial Fund Quarterly, Health and Society*, 51 (1973), pp. 271-317.

9.   N. Fuller, M. Patera, and K. Koziol, "Medicaid Utilization of Services in a Prepaid Group Practice Health Plan," *Medical Care*, 8 (1977), pp. 705-737.
10.   S. Greenfield, A. Komaroff, T. Paso, H. Anderson, and S. Nessim, "Efficiency and Cost of Primary Care by Nurses and Physicians Assistants," *New England Journal of Medicine*, 298 (1978), pp. 305-309; D. L. Sackett, W. O. Spitzer, M. Gent, and R. Roberts, "The Burlington Randomized Trial of the Nurse Practitioner: Health Outcomes of Patients," *Annals of Internal Medicine*, 80 (1974), pp. 137-142.

ACCESS TO CARE
AND EDUCATIONAL POLICY

A couple of decades ago we decided that the health needs of a metropolis required more medical intervention, and that with a little more intervention in health care we could cure if not prevent most health problems. So we said, Let us have more interveners, and we declared a doctor shortage. We said we needed 50,000 to 60,000 more doctors; we need twice as many as we have now. So we opened the flood gates of medical school, and out they poured.

But the doctors did not go where we wanted them to go. They did not go into primary care, and they did not go into the underdoctored areas. They continued to specialize, and they continued to go where they had always gone—to the suburbs. So rather than meeting health-care needs we encountered a dramatic escalation of health-care costs because doctors generate their own demand. Patients do not admit themselves to hospitals; they do not write prescriptions; and they do not order lab tests. In fact, 90 percent of all health-care costs results from decisions that doctors make. And people began to say, "We can't afford these people. They don't go where they are needed. We need to think of something else."

Then we started to talk about a service requirement. Some people said, We need a universal-service requirement. Others said, No, that is undemocratic, and you must remember that people go into medical school out of choice rather than by coercion. Some also said that a service requirement linked only to those who could not pay their tuition would be unfair, and so the struggle went. We could not get the doctors to go where we wanted, and we could not figure out a way to get them there.

Then we were into the post-Vietnam era, and we had medical-corps people coming back from Vietnam. And we said, "Aha, if the doctors won't do it, we will get someone else." We opened up programs all over the country to teach nonphysician medical practitioners to do what doctors could do, because we had come across the rather revolutionary notion that it didn't take a doctor to do most of the things that doctors do. Some of us had suspected that all along, but we had kept it a well-guarded secret.

The final evaluation of the distribution patterns of nonphysician practitioners is still coming off the typewriters and out of the computers, but preliminary results do not look too promising. We said it would be cheaper. Preliminary results show that the savings are not passed on to the taxpayer; they are not passed on to the fiscal intermediary; and they are not passed on to the user of services. The savings in so far as they are incurred accrue to the people who hire the paramedics. They go to the provider institutions or the providers, and so paramedics have not proved to be a cheap solution. Well, perhaps at least they went where doctors would not go. The preliminary results do not look too good there, either. The best we can hope for is a zero correlation between distribution and need for paramedical personnel. That is the very best we can hope for, and it looks very likely that just as physicians go to overdoctored areas so paramedics are also going to overdoctored areas. This has happened, I think, largely because of the remuneration system. Remuneration does not go to paramedics. They are legally dependent upon the physician or the provider institution. They are most likely to be hired by the provider institution or the provider that can most economically benefit from hiring them. Because of the peculiar structure of the medical care "market," this often has little relation to need. Thus paramedical personnel are located physically with the provider institution or the provider, and we have continued or even aggravated maldistribution.

So pouring out more doctors did not do it, and pouring out more paramedics has not done it, either. Both have further escalated health-care costs. I think that it is in this framework that we need to think about educational policy because we cannot just add more numbers. So educational policy has to be seen in the framework of trying to restructure and reform a system of health care that has grown like Topsy. We have to think not only about what we are doing but also about with whom we are working.

What types of people do we need to fill the slots and provide health care? That is, what types of people are most likely to provide primary care in underdoctored areas after they have been trained as physicians or paramedics? Minority medical applicants are much more likely than non-minorities to go to underserved urban areas and to enter primary care. Women are also several times more likely than men to enter primary care and to work in neighborhood health centers. Applicants from working-class backgrounds are several times more likely to enter primary care than are applicants from professional, managerial, and proprietal class origins. Similarly, applicants with primary-care work, human-service work, or face-to-face contact experience are several times more likely to enter primary care and to work in underserved areas than are applicants straight out of college or those who have worked primarily in research laboratories.

These, then, are the characteristics of people most likely to meet the health needs of tomorrow. How does this correspond to our actual selection process? My research at present is on the 40,506 current medical-school applicants, and our criteria for acceptance and rejection. Sixty-four percent of them are from professional, managerial, and proprietal origins compared to the less than 20 percent from these origins in the general population. Only 15 percent are from the working-class origins who comprise the majority of the male labor force in urban areas. Only 7 percent of medical enrollees are black, and that figure hasn't changed much in the last three or four years. There was a significant increase in black enrollees in the late sixties, but this has tapered and there is no evidence of further significant increases.

We also have a dramatic underrepresentation of medical enrollees from central cities and a corresponding overrepresentation of suburban youth. We likewise have a rather strange age bias on acceptance, which appears to be growing in the last decade. After the age of twenty-one, the chance of acceptance declines rather sharply. This indirectly penalizes persons who needed to work after college before applying to medical school and is more likely therefore to penalize working-class and minority applicants. We also provide no credit for human-services work experience and thus forfeit an excellent predictor of what type of a human being someone is going to be when providing human services.

What should we do? We need to greatly expand the use of what can be called the human instrument: evaluation of the human qualities of potential health-care providers by peers and by persons who will be receiving services from them. Instead, we are currently limited primarily to a paper-and-pencil evaluation which emphasizes undergraduate grades and medical-college admission test scores. The limitation of these indices is demonstrated by over two dozen studies in the last decade which show absolutely no correlation between physician performance, however measured, and medical-college entrance exams or undergraduate grades. Yet we continue to use them, in large part because of convenience. A ratio of ten applications for every opening means a lot of paperwork, and medical entrance test scores and grades are used as a convenient way of screening the applicants. The bottom half or two-thirds of all applications are merely discarded on this basis, often by a clerical employee.

To be sure, there is slight correlation between attrition in medical school and undergraduate grades. But part of this stems from the relative inflexibility of the medical-school curriculum, which largely prohibits learning at varied paces. A person with grave difficulty in one or two courses can fail, and must then either drop out of the system or repeat all courses for the entire year. However, attrition of this type can be decreased by using self-paced and self-instructional learning which permits varying course loads and rates of advance, and which permits students to tutor each other and/or tutoring by instructors or others. In fact, studies show that when students tutor other students, both groups learn more than studying by the traditional method.

The other correlation between medical-entrance exams, grades, and attrition is an inverse correlation with entering primary care. That is, those with the highest scores and grades are least likely to enter primary care and most likely to enter research or specialty clinical medicine. They are also least likely to go to underdoctored areas. Thus the use of academic indices as criteria for selecting people not only relies upon an invalid instrument but also selects precisely the types of applicants we least need: specialists, researchers, and suburban practitioners. We need to determine the level of scores and grades below which decreased performance may result, and beyond those levels utilize other criteria, criteria that assess human qualities and best predict later geographic and specialty distribution. This would increase the proportion of working-class and minority enrollees, probably increase the proportion of women, and certainly enroll a more mature class with human-services experiences. And these policies are relatively short-range and inexpensive.

The medium and long-range policies needed in medical education include a reduction in economic barriers to entry. Economic barriers for entering medical school or paramedical school are what my mother used to call "penny wise and dollar foolish." It costs $8,000 to $10,000 per year to maintain someone in a training program. That is a lot of money, but it costs between $50,000 and $60,000 per year to pay them later as physicians. If they go to the wrong place to practice, you are paying a lot of money for unnecessary health costs, physician-created demand, and iatrogenic disease. The cheapest time to maintain health professionals is while they are in school, and pinching there does not make sense. It is irrational precisely because the people who are most likely to meet the health-care needs of tomorrow cannot afford to get in.

The other thing to which we need give serious thought is some form of universal-service requirement, partly because of unmet needs but also because of the self-selective effect it has on admission. Perhaps physician-practitioner students in the program where I teach, who are unusually humanitarian, would not be there if they knew before they came that they had a one-or two-year service requirement. These are the ones least likely to enter primary care, those who can hardly wait to get to the suburbs, and who can hardly wait to end up in the surgical or a specialized emergency room. We have ten applications for every slot, plenty of people from which to choose, so we need not worry about the one-fourth that we might scare away. Let us instead concentrate on the people who are oriented toward providing the health-care needs that we have.

Finally, we need also to reconsider curriculum policies for health personnel. Only two-thirds of the medical schools have any ambulatory primary-care requirements. We are sending physicians out to give primary care, yet a third of the schools had no curriculum requirements to prepare them to do that. In addition, the majority of schools that do have the requirement have a rotation of less than two months. Practitioners are naturally reluctant to go out and provide services in an area where they feel incompetent. If you spend most of your time learning about lupus erythematosis but do not learn how to manage an outpatient diabetic, you are not going to feel comfortable managing common diseases in the community. Furthermore, the use of an exclusively technologic-intensive center for medical education fails either to develop adequately the highly skilled techniques of doing a medical history and a physical examination or the critical thinking necessary for diagnosis and care. Under current conditions the practitioner becomes overly dependent on the technology of the specialty hospital and not surprisingly feels more comfortable there. I think we need to change that. I think that half of the clinical curriculum time should be spent with outpatients. Persons providing primary care will spend 80 percent of their time with outpatients, and if they only spend

10 percent of it during medical school, they will be ill prepared to do so later.

So what about health care and the future of the metropolis? Well, I'm not really sure where we are going to be in the year 2000. But I think it really depends upon where we decide we need to go and, as they say in Kansas, "whether we're willing to bite the bullet to get there."

PART FOUR

CONCLUSION

PAULA DUBECK & ZANE L. MILLER

THE CONTEMPORARY
METROPOLITAN CRISIS

In the mid-twentieth century the outcome of intradisciplinary conflicts within the various social sciences, especially sociology, led to a decline in work on urbanization and community, the ascendance of quantification, and a more explicit concern with theory. These trends emerged from the ascendance of a mechanistic mode of thought which took individuals rather than social units, such as cities, as basic objects of study, and from the impact of relativism, drawn from physics, on the social sciences.[1] Together, the mechanistic mode of thought, the realization of the implications of the new relativism, and the quantitative revolution of the 1950s gave rise to a profound cynicism among social scientists about the possibility of determining cause-and-effect relationships and led them to follow the physicists in concentrating upon the discussion of "probabilities."[2] That gave impetus to the movement of the social sciences away from "applied" research and "reform" and into "pure" research and middle-range theory, and opened the way for the rise of "idealism" which in turn cleared the ground for the structural-functionalists and social systems theory.[3]

These events in the history of the social sciences in America happened at the same time and help account for the abandonment of the organic metaphor and the possibility of studying the city as a basic unit of society. The new research orientation in the social sciences, in short, created a theoretical context in which the city, not to mention the neighborhood or community, seemed merely an illusory construct that veiled the greater and "real" process of interaction among classes, associations, institutions, values, and norms. It largely left the study of the metropolis to the human ecologists, like R. D. McKenzie, Amos Hawley, and their students, who despite their attachment to biotic nomenclature, saw society in essentially mechanistic instead of organic terms and dealt with it through the quantitative analysis of the POET variables of population, (social) organization, environment, and technology, and to a handful of geographers and regional economists working in the tradition of Adna Weber and N. S. B. Gras. In the hands of community planners, the new view of metropolitan community denied the existence of cities as social communities. Instead, it treated the individual or family as the basic elements of urban society, as isolated units in neighborhoods or communities defined not by their propensity for social cohesion but by the fact that they constituted expedient areas for the delivery of convenient services, such as an elementary school or local shopping center, and access to a transportation network linking residential localities together and to the larger metropolis of jobs and leisure pursuits.

The long hot summers between 1964 and 1971, however, drove the social scientists back to the city, a place to which, by the logic of the 1950s, they could not go. The metropolis once more, as in the early twentieth century, seemed in crisis, and the revived general concern for cities emphasized the pathological aspects of urban life and the descent of urban society into a state of random disequilibrium, drift, and disorder. In some versions, the new outlook diagnosed metropolitan ailments as terminal. Lewis Mumford warned of the coming of necropolis—the city of the dead; Jane Jacobs built a career out of *The Death and Life of Great American Cities*; *Newsweek* ran a special issue on "Our Sick, Sick Cities;" city planners talked about constructing small new towns safely removed from the dangers of the exploding metropolises. Universities, spurred by the urgency of the crisis and the availability of federal funds, responded by returning to the urban field. The idea of the urban university came back into vogue, and centers and institutes for the study of urban problems, violence, poverty, and ethnicity proliferated. A host of social scientists from a variety of specialties made the term "interdisciplinary" an "in" word. Case studies, like Robert Dahl's work on New Haven politics and Gerald Suttles' on the social order of a Chicago slum, recovered some of their old legitimacy. And freshly minted Ph.D.'s in sociology, geography, economics, and political science unabashedly embellished their vitae with an urban specialty.

As the specialty flourished and diversified, methodological and theoretical disputes broke out. The popularity of urban studies among students, foundations, and the federal government created a kind of intellectual and ethical crisis in disciplines, especially sociology, which no longer saw the city as an appropriate unit of study,[4] and provided a fresh impetus for more optimistic work in community planning, public administration, the "policy sciences," and among that whole group of people we have designated the "urban professionals." Despite a decade of revived interest in urban studies, however, we stand now as skeptical about the legitimacy of the specialty and its theoretical under-pinnings as we do about the attempt under Presidents Johnson and Nixon to create a national urban policy.

A brief analysis of recent developments in the field of urban history helps to focus the crux of the difficulty. By the late 1960s urban historians were arguing over whether or not something deserving the appellation of the "new urban history" had developed. According to its proponents, the hallmarks of the genre consisted of concern with the poor and inarticulate, and a more sophisticated use of quantitative analysis. By the early 1970s a rough consensus on the issue began to take shape. The catalyst for the agreement came from the pen of Samuel P. Hays, who in 1972 criticized the new urban history for its atomistic tendencies. He caimed that "recent studies of geographical mobility and urban government have tended to turn thinking about cities toward concepts of individualization and homogeneity rather than toward patterns of variation and social structure." His paper included a survey of "some recent positive accomplishments toward a structural approach," and within five years Clyde Griffin argued that the Hays article had been influential in forging a rough consensus among social-science-oriented historians about the meaning of the "new urban history."

The consensus, in effect, denies that there is such a thing as urban history conceived as social history by arguing that we should be doing social-science history. Implicitly, if not explicitly, the proponents of urban history as social-science history seem to be moving toward the view of society that dominated the social sciences in the mid-twentieth century: their grand model of society seems mechanistic. It posits as its basic problem the task of finding the ways in which thousands or millions of individuals with conflicting desires, aspirations, values, and norms worked out a mutual accommodation for survival that produced a social order, and how one social order gives away to another. It is that formulation which threatens urban history with the same fate as urban studies among the social sciences, for it is that formulation which accounts for the stress on quantification and theory and the rejection of the neighborhood, city, or metropolis as an appropriate entity of study. Only macroanalysis in a given period of individuals or families, the fundamental units of society under the new conception, can reveal the hidden patterns among individuals and explain the operation of the social order in a precise and objectively measurable way.

Another and related question that deserves consideration among urban historians, social scientists, and "urban professionals" has been raised by Harold D. Woodman in a paper on the "new quantitative history." Woodman contends that "quantifiers," in their search for a precise specification of the problems they seek to resolve, are "forced to use modern statistics and mathematics applied to 'operational' social science theories. Since the term 'operational' as they use it means that it is a theory that can be mathematically and statistically quantified, the simple result is that the methodology dictates the problem rather than the other way around." Woodman obviously prefers a history which does it "the other way around," a "kind of history which does not . . . reject or ignore the potential insights of the social scientists but at the same time . . . does not . . . attempt to *become* a social science . . . . it seeks . . . to move from social history to a history of society" and it "offers no scientifically determined definitive answers." He objects not to quantification in history, but to quantitative history, and his objection may be worth thinking about among social scientists and urban professionals.

Equally important, however, the mechanistic formulation begs the critical question of whether society in historical or social-science perspective is in fact like nature in a biotic, mechanistic, or some other "natural" sense, and whether we cannot, as Richard C. Wade has advocated, devise an approach based on an appreciation of spatial, socio-economic, and political structure and process that makes the city or metropolitan area an appropriate unit of study without resorting to models postulating the operation of laws in human society, including those drawn from an analogue to relativity in physics. Pursuit of that route would probably lead historians and social scientists into a more serious consideration than apparent thus far of the utility of the work of Clifford Geertz, Peter Berger and Thomas Luckmann, and Gerald Suttles.

Geertz, for example, contends that culture began to take shape before humans finished the process of biological evolution, and that therefore our biological nature is the product of a continuous interplay between man-made culture and a physical environment shaped in part by human action. In this view, humans as we know them are in large part the creation of humans, historic beings at their very core. Similarly, Gerald Suttles in *The Social Construction of Community* argues for the social creation of territorial community, and Berger and Luckmann, in *The Social Construction of Reality*, contend that reality itself and therefore society is a fabrication of man. As Berger and Luckmann[5] put it,

our conception of the sociology of knowledge implies a specific conception of sociology in general. It does *not* imply that sociology is not a science, that its methods should be other than empirical, or that it cannot be "value-free." It does imply that sociology takes its place in the company of the sciences that deal with man *as* man; that it is, in that specific sense, a humanistic discipline. An important consequence of this conception is that sociology must be carried on in a continuous conversation with both history and philosophy or lose its proper object of inquiry. This object is society as a part of a human world, made by men, inhabited by men, and, in turn, making men, in an ongoing historical process. It is not the least fruit of humanistic sociology that it reawakens our wonder at this astonishing phenomenon.

These approaches, in short, take us back to Barry Karl's moral question of vision, and link it to theory.

Whether these kinds of questions and definitions get thrashed out by historians, social scientists, and urban professionals remains to be seen. The potential, at least, exists, for despite the appearance of a rough consens us on the new urban history, and despite the contradictory and self-critical attitudes that our Cincinnati sysmposia revealed among the urban professionals, differences of opinion range broadly enough and the sense of metropolitan crisis run strongly and persistenly enough to spark a stimulating discussion and reconsideration of where we stand with respect to moral, theoretical, and policy questions as we contemplate the future of the metropolis. The persisting sense of metropolitan crisis, the recent preparation for HUD by Amos L. Hawley and Vincent P. Rock of *Metropolitan America in Contemporary Perspective*, and the call in 1976 by political scientists David C. Leege[6] for a "contextual" approach to balance the behavioral emphasis of the 1950s and 1960s in political science, sociology, social psychology, and above all in economics, suggest that we may in fact stand on the brink of such a fundamental reconsideration. So, too, do the recent deliberations of the House Sub-Committee on the City.[7] In any case, it seems appropriate, and not very surprising, that as the United States proceeds through the last quarter of the twentieth century, both society at large and its urban professionals, as if in mute and intuitive ratification of the dictum that the past is past yet somehow impinges upon the present and the future, should be casting about for a new definition and for new modes of conceptualizing and ordering that evanescent thing which humans over the centuries have, with persistent stubornness, called the city.

NOTES

1.   As opposed to the kind of relativism associated with William James (who called it philosophical pluralism) and the pragmatists, which led, among other things, to the great debate among historians in the 1930s associated with the name of Charles A. Beard.

2.   John P. Diggins. *Up From Communism: Conservative Odysseys in American Intellectual History* (New York, 1975), pp. 121-31.

3.   See Robert Gutman and David Poponoe, *Neighborhood, City, and Metropolis: An Integrated Reader in Urban Sociology* (New York, 1970), pp. 3-6.

4.   Gutman and Poponoe, pp. 17-20.

5.   Peter L. Berger and Thomas Luckmann, *The Social Construction of Reality: A Treatise in the Sociology of Knowledge* (Garden City, N.Y., 1967), p. 189.

6.   David Calhoun Leege, "Is Political Science Alive and Well and Living at NSF: Reflections of a Program Director at Midstream," *PS* (Winter 1976), p. 15-16.

7.   Theodore Brown, "House Sub-Committee on the City," *Urbanism Past and Present*, Number 4 (Summer 1977), pp. 41-42.